PREHISTORIC ODISHA

PREHISTORIC ODISHA

(With Special Reference to Somakoi Basin)

RAJENDRA DEHURI

AGAM KALA PRAKASHAN
DELHI

First Published 2021

ISBN : 978-81-942937-6-7

Published by:
Dr. Agam Prasad, M.A., Ph.D., Diploma in Museology
For **Agam Kala Prakashan**
34, Central Market, Ashok Vihar
Delhi - 110 052
Tel.: 91-11-27212195, 43513480
Fax: 91-11-27212195
Email: agamkala101@gmail.com, agambook@yahoo.com
www.agamkala.com

Composed by:
Sushil Kumar
Delhi - 110 052
Mobile: 9891395309

Printed in India.

Dedicated
To
My Guru Prof. Kishor K. Basa

Contents

Prof. Byomakesh Tripathy
Vice-Chancellor

ଉତ୍କଳ ସଂସ୍କୃତି ବିଶ୍ୱବିଦ୍ୟାଳୟ
UTKAL UNIVERSITY OF CULTURE

FOREWORD

I am happy to introduce the book "prehistoric Odisha with special reference to Somakoi Basin" to the scholarly world as well as the general readers. The work is a novel attempt by the author to analyse prehistoric developments in Odisha. Earlier works on the subject have dealt with prehistoric culture of various parts of the State. The present work documents the earlier contributions in the field and at the same time, provides new materials in prehistoric scenario of Odisha, with special reference to Northern Odisha. The author has carried out extensive explorations in the Somakoi basin of district Keonjhar of Odisha.

Dr.Rajendra Dehuri has highlighted the prehistoric archaeology of North Odisha, with the help of field data, illustrations in the form of drawings, pai chart, photographs, tables with percentage of different stone tools and raw materials. During the field study, prehistoric as well as historical antiquities of the region were documented which are significant to understand the cultural sequence of the region.

Though lower paleolithics sites are few in number, a number of sites with upper Paleolithic artifacts, microlithic artifacts of Mesolithic period have been studied as components of flake and blade industry. A well developed blade technology is characterized of the Somakoi Basin. Neolithic sites, both finished and unfinished artefacts, are reported; the ring stone and axe are being the two dominant types of artifact.

The study has highlighted unknown cultural aspects of the region. I am sure, this work will be very helpful to scholars interested in archaeology and anthropology of Odisha in general and North Odisha studies in particular. The work is a welcome addition to Odishan studies.

(Prof.Byomakesh Tripathy)
Vice-Chancellor

Mobile : +91 8889192148
+91 8989986742
Email : vcuuc1@gmail.com

Sanskruti Vihar, Madanpur Bhubaneswar-752054, Odisha
Phone : 0674 - 2972311 (Off.) Email: mailboxuuc@gmail.com
Website : www.uuc.ac.in

Preface

The present work entitled *Prehistoric Odisha: With special reference to Somakoi Basin* attempts to provide a detail survey of the Palaeolithic, Mesolithic and Neolithic industries of the micro region taking into consideration to environmental adaptation of the prehistoric people and produced lithic implements of different prehistoric period. Interestingly, the survey area provide a wide variety of lithic assemblages so a trial trench also laid at Telkoi site to understand the cultural deposits and possibilities of draw paleo-cultural activities in North Odisha .

The North Odisha is well known for its archaeological evidences. There are number of prehistoric as well as historic sites reported from Keonjhar district. Because of closeness to the region and belongs to one of them I am very much interested to prepare the comprehensive data. This is quite a modest attempt to reconstruct the archaeological prospect of North Odisha. The archaeological remains clearly imply that the area shows a sequence from Lower Palaeolithic to Neolithic period, in which sites with the Microliths and Neolithic or ground stone tools are more numerous.

The present work forms a part of the M. Phil assignment and has taken the present shape by the help and inspiration of many benevolence minds and hands. It is my prime responsibility to express and acknowledge such help and contributions.

While completing this stupendous task, I owe my indebtedness to Prof. S.K. Ghoshmaulik (Retd.), the then head of the Department of Anthropology for giving opportunity to under take the field work. Again I owe my gratitude to all my teachers of Post Graduate Department of Anthropology, Utkal University, Bhubaneswar for their moral support.

I am grateful to Prof. K.C. Tripathy (Retd.), for his encouragement, sincere guidance, valuable advice and keen interest without which it would not have been possible for completing this work.

Words are very poor to express my deep sense of gratitude to my guide Prof. Kishore K. Basa, whose restless effort, timely guidance and effective advice chanalised me in the direction of materializing on the present work.

I also acknowledge indebtedness to Mr. Daitari Sahoo, Senior Lecturer, Department of Anthropology for his valuable suggestions and encouragement from time to time. Thanks to Dr. Basanta Mohanta, Mr. Tapan Kumar Das, Dr. Jitu Mishra, for their valuable suggestions and guidance during and after fieldwork. I am very much thankful to Mr. Purna Chandra Baskey, Mrs. Panaswari Murmu and Mr. Shyama Ranjan Hembrum for their helps during the field work. The maps and drawings of antiquities have been prepared by Mr. Raman Kumar, Draftsmen, Archaeological Survey of India, Excavation Branch-III, Patna for which I am profoundly grateful. I am very much thankful to the staff members of the Excavation Branch-III, Patna, especially Mr. Ashish Kumar, Dr. Niraj Kumar Mishra, Dr. Virendra Kumar and Mr. Dinesh Kumar Yadav for his co-operation in the hours of need.

I am grateful to Dr. Arakhita Pradhan for his constant encouragement and scholarly interaction in the subject, analysis the findings, go through the draft and made necessary rectification wherever required and benefited by his keen observations.

I am especially thankful to my uncle and aunt Mr. Digamber Dehuri, Mrs. Sandhyarani Dehuri and friends Mrs. Sushree Samparna Mishra, Mr. Prabin Tripathy for their help during course of the work.

I am also thankful to my parents Shri Bira Dehuri and Smt. Sabitri Dehuri for their inspiration and support. My wife Aparna has given me all moral and emotional support and has stood by me in every difficult situation while preparing the book and hence she deserves my sincere thanks. Thanks to my son Arya Vedant Dehuri and daughter Ananya Abhipsa Dehuri for their support and encouragement.

Shri. Khirod Chandra Behura, Mrs. Monika Negi and Shri. Dhiraj Singh have taken enough pain to type out the present work neatly. I am extremely thankful to them.

I am indeed greatful to Dr. Agam Prasad for showing interest in my work and publishing it. A special thanks to Shri Ashok Kumar Pandey and staff of Agam Kala Prakashan, New Delhi. Lastly, but not least I am grateful to those authors of different books, journals, articles and reports which I have consulted for constructing the work.

Patna **Rajendra Dehuri**
Date: 17 Oct, 2020

List of Tables

List of Illustrations

Figures

Plates

CHAPTER 1

INTRODUCTION

Research in Indian prehistory has travelled a long way since the first discovery of prehistoric relics by Robert Bruce Foote in 1863. Research in stone age archaeology which is filled up with the arrival of H.D. Sankalia on the scene, since then researches in the field of Indian prehistory have passed through many developments in the methodogical and interpretational phases. There has been growing emphasis on quantitative and qualitative analysis of stone age artefacts and from the 1960s extensive use of statistic is being made in the field of prehistoric archaeology (Mishra 1992, Jacobson 1979). The prehistoric archaeology study is drastic change in India since the 1970s, as a corollary to the new advancements, made in other parts of the world, in methodology and theoretical interpretations.

The Indian sub-continent shows varied geographical settings in respect of land forms, vegetation, drainage system etc. The fundamental assumption which has been realised is that man is a part of the environment (natural and social) and that his behavioural patterns (explicated by an appraisal of archaeologically visible residue of human behaviour) reflect his adoptative strategies in time and space. Moreover, it has now became a common practice to subject an archaeological site for intensive investigations to enumerate the sum total of human behaviour, land use patterns, exploitative strategies, dietary habits and the possible types of social organization. Fortunately, in the Indian context, parallels for such an explication can be drawn from the various tribal groups whose occupational zones, quite often are contiguous with the stone age habitats stone Age studies in the Indian subcontinent since the last two decades have established on firm grounds for the temporal spatial distribution of Lower, Middle, and Upper Palaeolithic and Mesolithic period respectively. Indian prehistorians have been focusing attention to evaluate the interaction of man with the environments and the variation within a cultural system (called micro variation) by investigating a single geographical unit at the micro level. This has been adopted in the last one decade by many prehistorians (Mishra 1973, Jacabson 1975, Murty 1982, Paddaya 1982 and Cooper 1983).

Against this background the author has investigated the Somakoi basin in Keonjhar district Odisha, and attempted to show the cultural remains and behavioural patterns of the prehistoric people within a well-defined eco-system. The study area constitutes eco-zones with characteristic land forms, flora and fauna and drainage systems.

The aim of the present study on the one hand, is to reconstruct the succession of cultural variation (Typo-technologically with cultural system) distribution pattern etc., and on the other hand geo-archaeological ground as taken this natural land form, their tributary and drainage of the region, adopting the approach of geo-archaeological analogy.

Among the previous research in the field of prehistory of Odisha, the contribution of N. K Bose and D. Sen (1958), G.C Mohapatra (1962), K.C Tripathy (1972), R.N Das (1967), P.K Singh (1984), P. K Behera (1992), P. Mahanty (1989), S.C Nanda (1984) and Roy (1993), B. Mahanta (2003) are noteworthy in the prehistoric cultural succession of the state. Their works opened new avenues for further research on various facets of prehistoric Odisha. Within the broader frame work of prehistoric cultural succession established by the above mentioned authors, the present author conducted micro level investigations, of a geographical area, which approximately covers about 50 sq km.

These investigations brought to light Palaeolithic, Mesolithic and Neolithic sites, as a result of intensive survey of a limited geographical area and interpretation of the data on the basis of typo technologically.

PHYSIOGRAPHY OF ODISHA

The state of Odisha located on the eastern coast of India, lies between 17°48’ and 22°34’ N latitude and 81°24’ and 87°29’ E longitude. It is bounded on the north by Jharkhand, on south by Andhra Pradesh, on the west by Chhatisgarh and on the north-east by West Bengal and bay of Bengal on the east.

Geographically the state is divided into four distinctive regions.

1. Northern plateau,
2. Central river basin
3. Coastal plains, and
4. Eastern ghats.

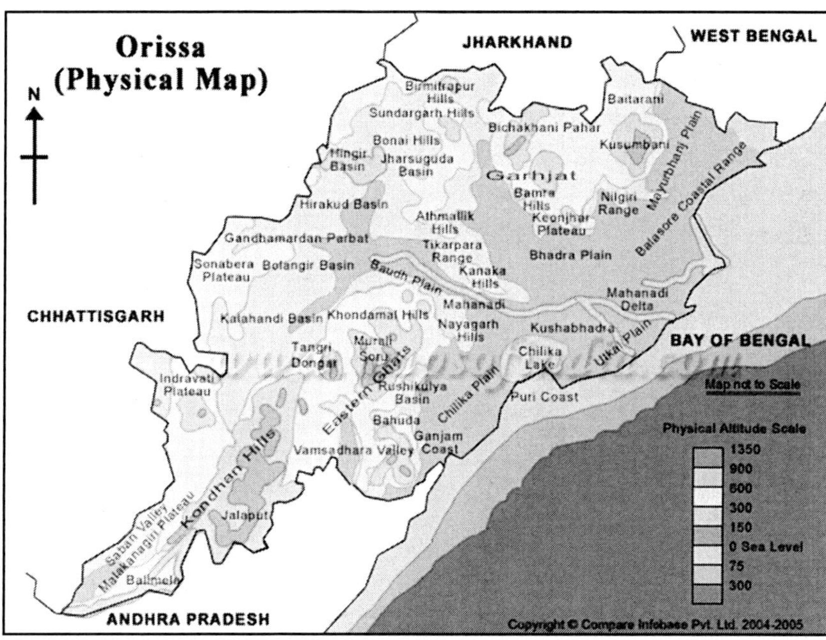

Fig-1: Physical map of Odisha (Courtesy: CIPL)

The northern plateau covers the district of Mayurbhanj, Keonjhar and Sundargarh and Pallahara sub-division of Angul district. It is undulating up-land, frequently interpreted by hill ranges and rivers. It is a continuation of the Chotanagpur plateau of Jharkhand. The average elevation of the plateau in the central region is 914 m.

The central river basin lies between the northern plateau and eastern hills and comprises the water shed areas of the principal river of the state, namely the Mahanadi, the Brahmani and the Baitarani. The three river valleys run almost parallel to each other. Isolated hills rising abruptly from the plains are a frequent sight in this tract.

The coastal plains of Odisha stretch from the Subarnarekha in the north to the Rushikulya in the south. The coastal region has been formed by the six major rivers which bring silt from their catchments. The six major rivers are the Subarnarekha, the Brahmani, the Budhabalanga, the Baitarani, the Mahanadi and the Rushikulya. The coastal plain cover most of the districts of Balasore, Bhadrak, Kendrapara, Jagatsinghpur, Jajpur, Cuttack and Puri are sandy whereas Jagatsinghpur, Kendrapara and Cuttack are swampy and marshy. There are a series of hill ranges of heterogeneous composition, which stretch from the northern border of Odisha through the coastal region of Andhra Pradesh to join Nilgiri in the western part of Tamilnadu. They cover Koraput, Malkangiri, Kalahandi, Rayagada, Phulbani, Gajapati and Ganjam districts. The average elevation is 762 m. and the highest peak is the Deomali (1.607 m.) of Koraput. The eastern hills comprise wide upland plateau with forest.

ADMINISTRATIVE UNITS

Odisha assumed the position of a state in 1936, when it comprised six districts (Cuttack, Balasore, Puri, Sambalpur, Ganjam, and Koraput). Presently the state is divided into 30 revenue districts.

People:- According to 2011 census, the population of Odisha was 36,804,660. The coastal tract is more thickly populated than the inland areas. The least populated areas are the Eastern Ghats.

Fig-2: Administrative map of Odisha.

On the basis of the 2011 census Odisha has tribal population of 9,590,756 which is about a little over 24 percent of the total population of the state. Odisha ranks second in the number of tribal population with 62 tribes represented. Among the religious groups, Hindus constitute the majority. They are followed by Muslims, Christians, Sikhs, Jains and Buddhists.

PHYSIOGRAPHY OF KEONJHAR

The district Keonjhar lies between 21°1' N and 22° 10'N latitude and 85°11'E and 86°22' E longitude. The district is bounded on the north by the district of West Singhbhum in Jharkhand, on the east by the districts of Mayurbhanj, Bhadrak and Balasore, on the south by the districts of Jajpur and Dhenkanal and on the west by the districts of Angul and

Sundargarh. The district consists of a compact area and its extreme length from north to south is nearly 145 km. and the average breadth from east to west is about 65 km. It is divided into two widely dissimilar tracts, the lower Keonjhar and the upper Keonjhar. The former is a region of valleys and low lands, while the later includes mountains highlands with general slope from north to south. The highlands consisting of clusters of rugged crags offered a safe retreat to its inhabitants in troubles times. The mountain tops appear from the low lands to be sharply ridged or peaked, but in reality they have extensive tablelands on their summits, fit both for pasture and for tillage. The average elevation in its central part is about 500 m. At places, isolated wills rise abruptly from the plains. But most of the areas have a general elevation of over 600 m, which forms the watershed of some rivers.

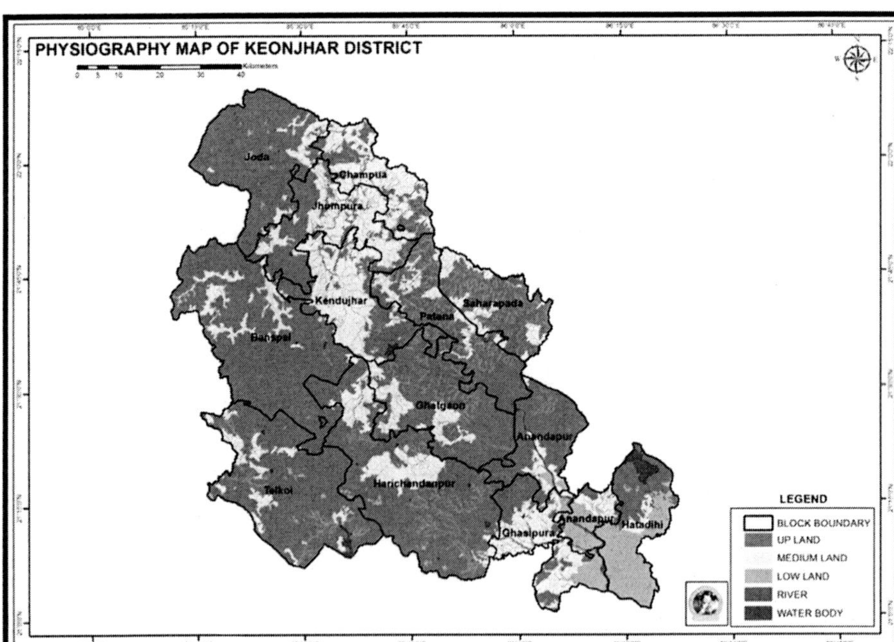

Fig-3: Physiography map of Keonjhar district.

SUB-DIVISIONS, TAHSILS AND POLICE STATIONS

The district is divided into three sub-divisions, seven Tahasils and fifteen police stations. The sub-division of this district is big in size and population. In 2011 census in a sub-division area has a population of not more than 8,75,000. The largest and the most populated among the sub division is Keonjhar with population of 8,71,927 and population of Anandapur subdivision has 4,62,439, while the Champua sub-division is the population having only 4,67,369 inhabitants in 2011. Each sub-division consists of two or more police station area and tahsil. In all, there are 14 police stations in the district.

TOPOGRAPHY

(a) NATURAL DIVISION:

The district is mostly covered with dense jungles and a long range of hills. The region is undulating and a long ranges of hills. The district is undulating and contains a number of valleys and soil varies from a rich loam to the gravely slopes. The Baitarani river takes its rise in the hilly north western division.

A wide range of lofty hills and dense Jungles from the boundary between Keonjhar and the neighbouring district of Dhenkanal is significant one. From the eastern side of this ranges a large plateau extends to Mayurbhanj and Singhbhum on the one hand to the borders of lower Keonjhar on the other, varying in height from 244 to 457 meter. With the exception of isolated hills and undulating tracts, this vast plateau is generally open and occupied by large villages and number of hamlets; it is well watered by streams which in the rains are raging torrents hurrying to discharge their waters into Baitarani. The range of hills in which the Baitarani rises, develops on the south-east into lofty peaks and wide ridges till it strikes the Sukinda, in the Jajpur district. Below this belt towards the east is the lower Keonjhar comprising Anandapur sub-division and a portion of Keonjhar sub-division. For the first 16 km., this tract emerges slope from the belt of hills and then spreads out into an open plain towards Jajpur district flanked by two long ranges of hills to Sukinda and Mayurbhanj borders. This tract is similar to the adjoining districts Balasore, Bhadrak and Jajpur containing little jungle and is dotted with a few low isolated hills. It is well cultivated and thickly populated.

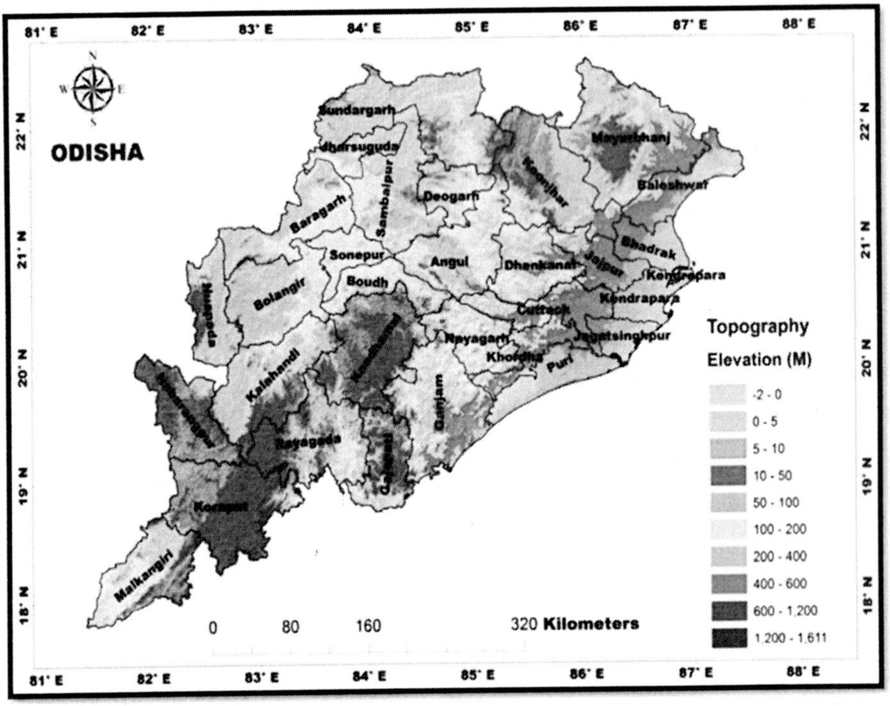

Fig-4: Topographic map of Odisha

The crescent-shaped watershed which runs from north to the south is the home of the primitive tribes, chiefly the Bhuiyans and the Juangs. Through the valleys consist of rich alluvial soil, the uplands consist mainly of detritus gravely slopes and thereby hill streams which eventually discharge their waters into Brahmani.

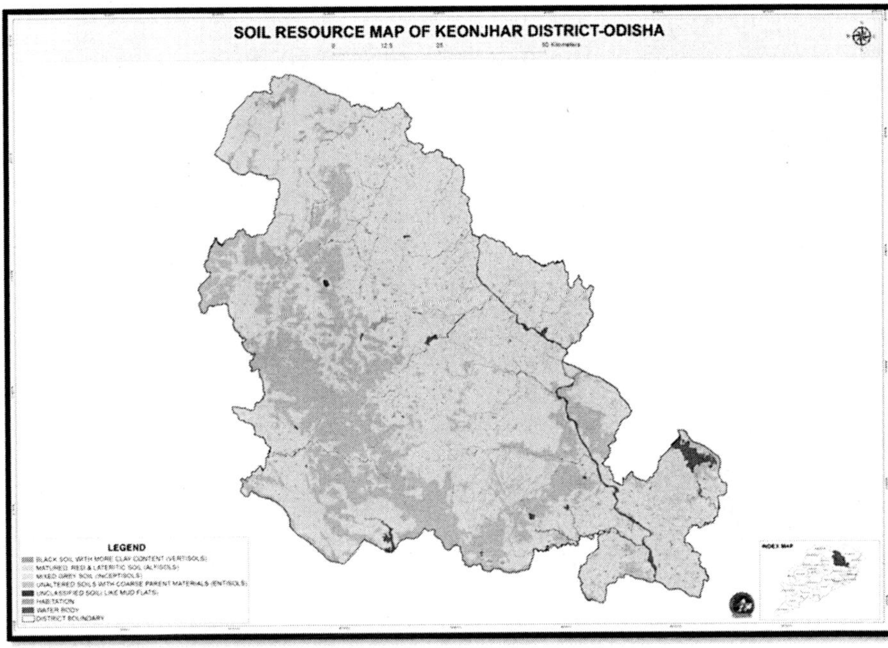

Fig-5: Soil resource map of Keonjhar district.

b) MAIN PEAKS:

The principal peaks are Gandhamardan (1.060 m.) about 10 km. from the headquarters with a wide ridge on the top, Mankadanacha (1.177 m.) on the Bonai border, Gonasika (978 m.), Thakurani (915 m.), Tomka (785 m.), Bolat (554 m.), Khajaru (9.18 m.), Ranga (897 m.), Mahaparabat (716 m.), Khandadhar Parbat (915 m.) situated near the border of Bonai and Pallahara and Sitabinji (670 m.) situated at a distance of 19 km from Keonjhar district headquarters in an eastern direction. Chakratirtha or Baula Parbat is situated at a distance of 16 km. from Anandpur in north-eastern direction.

(c) MAIN RIVER AND THEIR TRIBUTARIES

The rivers of the districts emerge out of the hilly tracts into the plain country with great velocity and are charged with large volumes of water during monsoon. In summer, they become almost dry. Their beds are usually rocky which render them unfit for navigation. There are a large number of hill streams in the district which form the major water resources.

BAITARANI

The river Baitarani is the largest river of the district. It rises from the Keonjhar sub-division among the hills in the south-west of the district and flows to north as a hill stream until the Singhbhum border where it abruptly turns to the south. It forms during part of its course the boundary between this district and Mayurbhanj for certain distance. In the dry season the river is navigable by small boats, but with difficulty. Important places located on its banks are Anandapur, Champua, Rajnagar, Udaypur, Fakirpur, Balibarua and Habeleswar. Almost every year in the rainy season the river is heavily charged with flood water. At a distance of about 40 km from Karanjia (in Mayurbhanj district) there occurs a deep pool in the river Baitarani known as Bhimkund.

ARADEI OR ORORAI

The Aradei or Ororai rises in the hill regions near Bararoan Pahar in the south-east of Keonjhar and flowing northward meets with the Machhakandana river about 3 km. south of Palasapanga, it then proceeds further in a northern direction and meets the river Baitarani about 8 km. south of Champua. The other tributaries of Aradei are Kadai and Sothi or Kasia which are two important hill stream of the district.

KANJHARI

The Kanjhari rises in the hills near about Gonasika and flowing in a north-eastern direction meets with the Baitarani south of Udayapur.

It is about 56 km in length and important villages like Ramachandrapur, Raghunathpur and Poipani and situated near its bank.

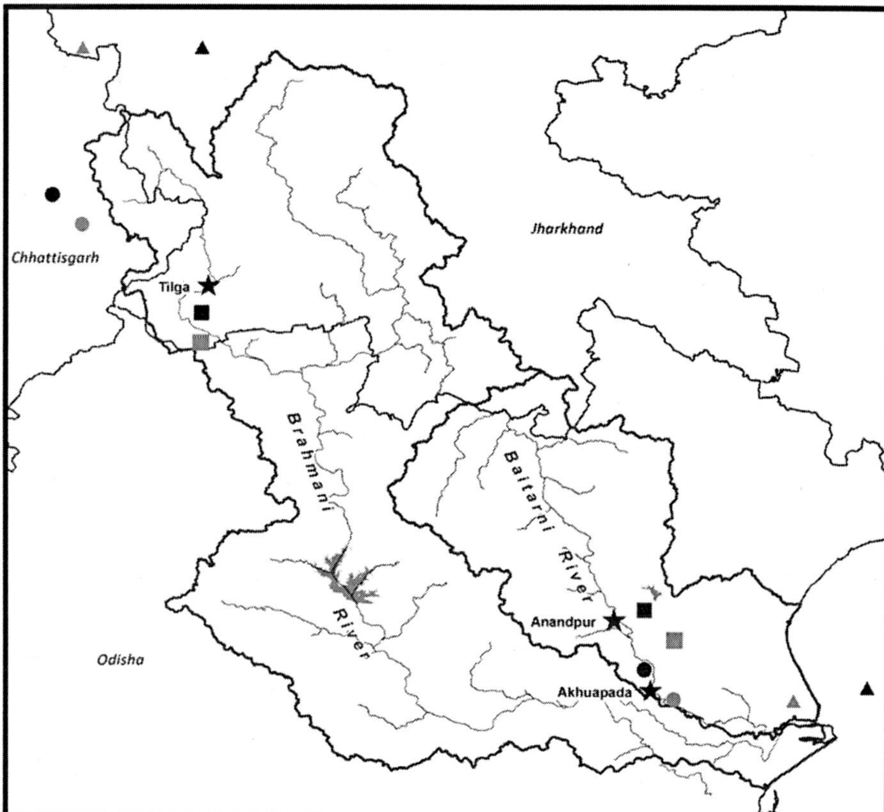

Fig-6: Drainage system of Brahmani and Baitarani basin.

SEETA

The Seeta takes it rise in the Sarupata hill situated near Dhenkikote. After flowing about 16 km it meets the river Kukurkata.

KUKURKATA

It rises in the forest near Jhalbera and flowing in easterly direction falls into the river Baitarani. It is about 32 km. in length and flows through densely wooded tract. Some important relics of historical interest are found in its upper valley. The noteworthy relics being those of fresco paintings and inscriptions at Dangaposi and Sitabinji.

KUSAI

The Kusai rises from the Rebna Reserved forests south of Meghanada Parbat and flows in south-eastern direction till it meets the river Kukurangi. Then it takes almost an easterly direction and follows a zigzag course until it finally debouches into the river Baitarani. Its important tributaries are Remal, Sendhei and Ganda. On the bank of the river is located the village Deogaon which is famous for the temple of Kosaleswar Siva of the mediaval period.

MUSAL

The Musal rises in Meghanad Parbat. Flowing for a certain distance due north it abruptly turns east and south-east and then debouches into the Baitarani near Simia. It receives tributes from numerous hill-streams during its 53km. course in the district.

MACHHA KANDANA

The Machha Kandana rises in Bararaon Pahar south of Keonjhar, flows in an almost northerly direction and meets the Aradei north of Keonjhar.

KARO

The Karo rises in the Bonai sub-division in the Sundargarh district and enters into Keonjhar from the north-western corner of Champua sub division and flows towards West Singhbhum in Jharkhand. The town of Barbil is situated on its bank.

SALANDI

The Salandi rises in the Similipal hills of Mayurbhanj district. It enters the district of Keonjhar at Champapal village, there from taking a south-eastern course it flows about 19 km. inside Padhiaipalli and Soso area and finally falls into the river Baitarani in Bhadrak sub-division. The average width of the river is about 30 m. The important villages situated on its bank are Soso and Balibarai.

BRAHMANI

It is the largest river which originated from the Chotanagpur plateau by primarily two rivers called south Koel and Sankh and both have joined together near Panposh in Sundargarh district and from downward called as Brahmani. The Brahmani has also the usual religious sanctity attached to it which has received recognition in some Puranas. The name Brahmani appears to be a modern one but its old name is Sankhajyoti. The Brahmani enters Angul district 3 km. west of Banor in Pallahara sub-division. In south ward the river marks the border of Pallahara and Talcher sub-division. The Brahmani is 799 km long and there are 45 major tributaries.The Somakoi, Tikra, Singlajor, Nigra and Ramaila are major tributaries of Brahmani which join with the river at different places. It has a catchment area of about 39,033 square kilometres in Odisha alone. The river has uncertain course which changes occasionally but generally it flows in south ward direction and then finally drain into Bay of Bengal. The length of the river within Angul district is about 75 km. Apart from these above tributaries the river Brahmani has a number of other tributaries in lower part.

MANKARA

It takes its origin in Sadar sub-division of Keonjhar district then flows west ward. The Kukhra or Kakharua is the major tributary of this river which joins about 7 km. east of Pallahara.

TIKRA

The River Tikra rises in Rairakhol (Redhakhol) sub-division of Sambalpur district and after passing through a portion of Deogarh sub-division enters into the Angul district and joins river Brahmani near Kaniha.

NIGRA

It rises from the hills which forms the boundary between Angul and Athamallik sub-divisions, joins the Brahmani at Kharga Prasad near Meramandali railway station in Dhenkanal sub-division. The Nigra has two principal tributaries known as Bauli and Mutkuria with a length of 48 km. and 45 km. respectively.

SOMAKOI

The river Somakoi takes its origin near Gendachaua hill of Kalapat reserved forest area of Keonjhar district. It follows a zigzag course almost in a westerly direction and falls into the river Brahmani in Angul district. Telkoi, one of important place is situated on its bank. Its length is about 50 km. in Angul district.

(d) FLORA

The forest are of monsoon type and classified as (a) Tropical moist deciduous forest and (b) Tropical semi-evergreen forest. The Sal *(Shorea Robusta)* forest with mixed community of species represents the climatic climax where the dry deciduous vegetation and thorny xerophytic communities characterise various stages of degradation or edaphic climaxes. Within these broad divisions of monsoon forest occur characteristic vegetation types depending upon local habitat or niche.

The principal species found throughout the district is Sal *(Shorea robust).* The more important associates of Sal are Asian *(Termilia tomentosa),* Amla *(Phyllanthus amblica),* Bahara *(Terminalia beterica),* Gambhari *(gmelina arbarea),* Givinga *(guaama tomestosa),* Harida *(Terminalia chebula),* Jamun *(eugenic Jobbolana),* Kendu *(Diopyrosemporpteris),* Kumbhi *(arborea),* Kusum *(Adina Cordifolia),* Kusum Caveya *(Cavthamustistorices),* Piasal *(Piero carpus marsupium),* Sisoo *(Dalbergiasisoo),* Sunari *(Cassio fistual),* Kangra *(xyiladolabiformis)* and Rai *(Dilleniapentagyna).* Bamboo is another important associate of Sal. Teak, not naturally in the locality has been successfully introduced in the forest of Keonjhar district. As in new plantation basis, Eucalyptus and Acacia more found mix with Sal forest.

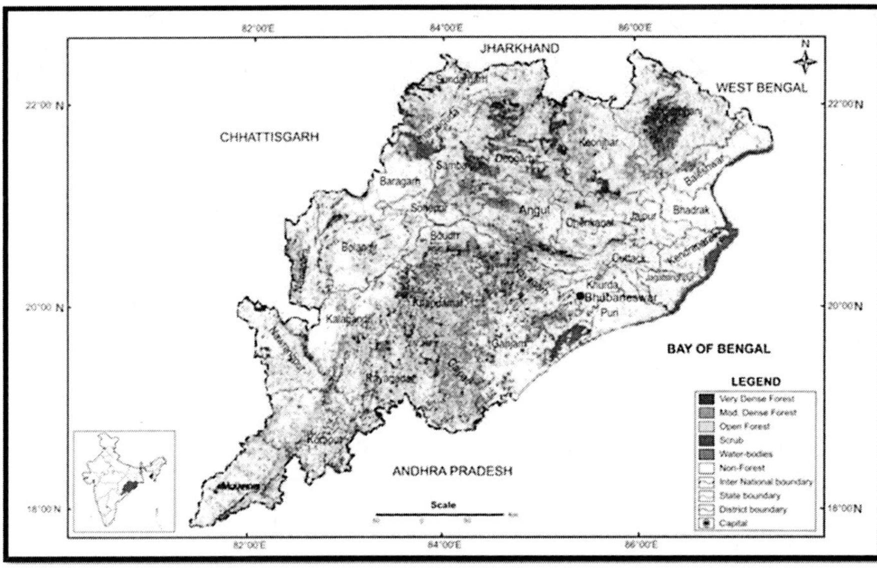

Fig-7: Forest map of Odisha

The aesthetic value of some species is also noteworthy. Among the ornamental plants and trees found in the district are Palasa or flame of forest *(Butia frondosa),* Ashoka *(Sarala India),* Champa *(Michila Champaca),* Krushna Chuda *(Dalnonie Regina),* Simul *(Bombay mela buricum),* Bharima *(Kydia Calycina),* Kanchana *(Bahaunia Varieget), peltopherun pieno carpum* and *Asia fistula.*

A fern *(Cyathea Spinulosa)* generally occurring in monsoon forest is found in Keonjhar district. The 'Birds nest' fern (*Drynaria quercifolia*) and many Epiphytes like *pyrrosia adnascnes* (fern) *Dendrobiam sp. cymbidium* and Aerides species of orchids occur and indicate humid tropic conditions and primeval forest.

(e) FOUNA

The extensive and dense forests of the district harbour a great number of wild animals, viz-Elephants, Leopards, wild Pigs & Bears. The carnivorous animals includes Tiger *(Panthera tigris),* Kalarapatria Bagha *(Panthera pardus),* Heta Bagha *(Hyaena Hyaena),* Bilua *(Canis aureus),*

Salia Patini (*Viverricula Indica),* Kuji Neula *(Harpestes auropunctatus),* Odha *(Lutra perspicillata),* Bhalu *(Melursus Ursinus),* and ungulates like Hati *(Elephas maximus),* Sambar *(Cervus unicolor niger),* Chital *(Axis axis),* Kutra *(Muntiacus muntjak),* Khuranti *(Moschiolamemina),* and Barha *(Sus scrota cristutus)* all herbivorous. The common class of rodents like Nepali Musa *(Ratufa Indica),* Gunduchi Musa *(Funambulus Pennanti),* Jhinka *(Hystrix Indica Indica)* Tekua *(Lepus nigricollis),* Musa *(Tateraindica),* Gatua Musa *(Bandilota bengalensis)* are often met with while Bajrakapta *(Manis crassicaudataaurita)* is rare. Monkeys *(Hanuman and pati)* are quite common and are seen in the villages in the periphery of the reserved forest.

Like the wild animals, bird life is also plentily available in the district. The Peafowl *(Faro cristatus),* Jungle fowl *(Gallus gallus)* and Spur fowl *(Galloerdixspadicea)* are numerous. In cold weather flocks of geese, ducks and teal are found in swampy lands and reservoirs. The whistling teal and the little cotton-teal are common residents. The pigeons, open billed stork, the Indian pond heron and the Bhrungraj a rare species, are also met with.

The poisonous snakes like Cobra, Resells viper, Krait and non-poisonous; Python, Dhomano, Dhanda, Kandanali are commonly found in this district. The principal fish are Rohi *(Lobeo rohita),* Mirkali *(Cirrhina mrigala),* Bhakur *(Catla catla),* Sal *(Ophicephalus marulius)* and Seal *(Ophicephalus striatus)* besides, a large number of other varieties are also found.

(f) GEOLOGY:

The district is favoured with vast deposit of mineral wealth such as Iron Ore, Manganese and Chromite. The Singhbhum- Keonjhar – Bonai belt passes through the district and continue 48 km. Altogether out of which 14.5 km. of this belt falls in the district. The resources of Iron Ores are more than 2500 million tonnes. The main places of Iron Ore deposits are Thakurani, Joda, Banspani, Sasangada and Gandhamardan Hills. Manganese Ores are found more than 20 million tonnes at Koida, Barbil, Bhadrasahi, Joda, Kalimati etc. The grade of Ores varies from 32% to

80% chromite is also available at Nuasahi and Boula in the district having a quantity of more than 6 million tonnes. Besides, the above minerals, pyrophilite and Dolomites are also available in this district. Pyrophilite deposits are found in Keonjhar sadar, Harichandanpur and Banspal Blocks having quantity more than 8 million tonnes. Dolomite deposits are found in Joda Block.

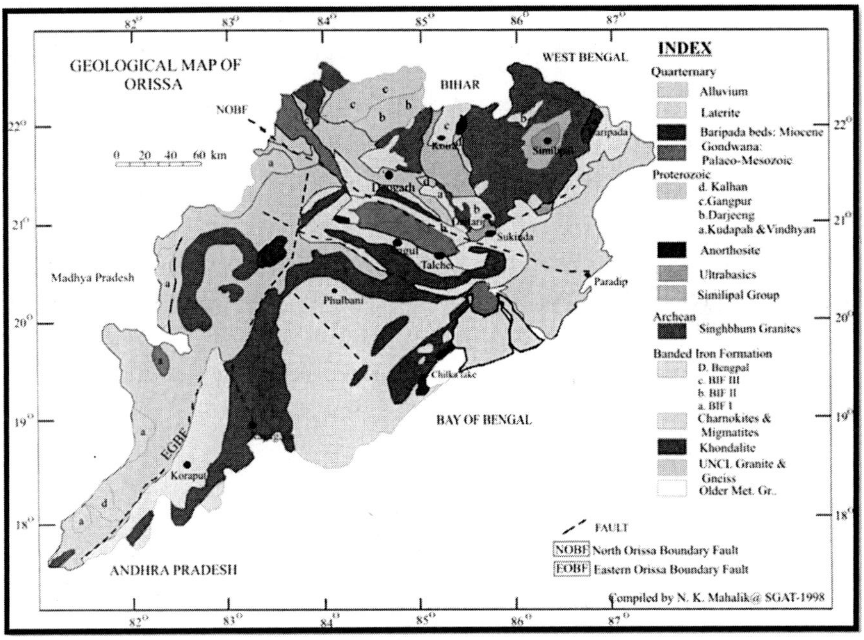

Fig-8: Geological map of Odisha

(g) CLIMATE

The climate of Keonjhar is characterised by an oppressive hot summer, high humidity and well distributed rainfall during the monsoon season. The year may be chiefly divided into four seasons, the hot season lasts from March to May, and the period from June to September is the south-west monsoon season. October and November constitute the post monsoon season and the cold season is from December to February.

PREVIOUS RESEARCH

The earliest discovery of Palaeolithic artefacts in Orissa was made nearly a century ago by V. Ball from Angul (Kaliahota), Talcher (Harichandanpur), Dhenkanal and Sambalpur (Barsuapali) (Ball 1875: 76-80). P. Acharya (1923-24) and R.D. Banerji (1930) reported Palaeolithic from Baidipur in present day Mayurbhanj district. In 1939 N.K. Bose and his colleagues discovered additional stone implements of Lower Palaeolithic from the same region. Acharya and Worman reported a number of Palaeolithic sites from Baripada region in Mayurbhanj district in 1939 (Bose and Sen. 1948).

However, systematic research in the prehistory of Odisha began around 1940. In this phase N.K. Bose and D. Sen excavated a few sites at Kuliana in Mayurbhanj and discovered Lower Palaeolithic in lateritic deposit. This was followed by the investigation of Bose and Sen (1948:195,1958) in Mayurbhanj. The implement sites brought to light by them are Baripada, Brahmana gaon, Bhuasuri, Kakaberia, Kamta and Kuliana. All are open air Lower Palaeolithic sites located on the banks of the river Burhabalanga. The Mayurbhanj Industry as defined by them is a core dominated Industry with choppers followed by the bifaces, a few cleaver and having a small admixture of flakes showing cruder workmanship. Between 1956-59 G.C Mohapatra carried out a systematic exploration in the valleys of the river Mahanadi, Brahamani and Burhabalanga in the northern districts Dhenkanal, Sundargarh, Sambalpur, Keonjhar, and Mayurbhanj of Odisha. His work brought to light a succession of prehistoric cultures in Odisha.

During late 50's and early 60's quite a few isolated discoveries of stone age have been reported microliths from Kaniha in Talcher. Sub-division by Ghosh (1958-59:36), Boramandar, Banaikala, Danguaposi in Keonjhar district by Mitra (1961-62: 36-37). From Tel and its tributaries and form the districts Bolangir, Ganjam, Kalahandi by Raghunath (1963-64 :27) a few microliths from Vani Vihar in Bhubaneswar by Das (IAR 1963-64: 90) and from Bolangir by Mukharjee (1968-69 : 68).

The work of Tripathy (1972) during the early 70's gave a footing to the Mesolithic culture along with Lower and Middle Palaeolithic cultural evidences from Tel river basin.

P.K. Singh 1985 explored 53 Palaeolithic sites in the Dhenkanal district of central Odisha. They are mainly hand axes and Cleavers as the predominant types, some of these being associated with lower pebbly gravel & kankarised soil, quartz and quartzite are the main raw materials.

Apart from these sites a Neo-chalcolithic site Sankerjang was excavated by the State Archaeology Department, Government of Odisha. The important of Sankerjang lies not only in material recovery such as ground stone axes, adzes, copper bangles and small tools as well as human skeletal remains and teeth, but also having yielded the first Rodiocarbon date for Odishan archaeological site.

P.K. Mohanty's noteworthy work around Keonjhar Mesolithic site yielded microliths in Keonjhar. P.K. Behera reported Neolithic sites in Keonjhar at Bonaigarh and Sulabdiha. These sites are important for northern Odisha Prehistoric studies.

Ranjana Roy of Calcutta University in her field session 1992-93 reported another metal age site at Kuanr and Neolithic site at Pallahara region. The first one may be considered as Chalcolithic because of nine bangles and two rings of copper, second one is located both side of the Mankara river, artefact include axes, adzes, ring stone, chisel, side scraper, blade, waste flake, and potsherds.

Arakhita Pradhan reported few sites with palaeolithic, mesolithic and neolithic tools in Rairakhol Tehsil in Sambalpur district and Athamallik Tehsil in Angul district (IAR 1996-97)

Apart from this, the Department of Anthropology, Utkal University, Bhubaneswar has conducted a field work every year.

This geographical location, ecological setting, natural resources and available findings throw light on the presence of past cultures.

With this background it is appropriate to discuss the study area with site description is the content of the next chapter.

CHAPTER 2

STONE AGE SITES IN THE SOMAKOI BASIN

Archaeology is a source of history; it is concentrated in sites as well as the past human activity. It might consist of a quarry, a trail, a burial, so that some traces of the activity are to be found. Hence, a systematic exploration of the site is the logical start to the archaeological investigation of given region. It attempts to locate as many of sites as possible to assess their nature and importance through surface exploration and the collection associated artefacts and to produce an adequate record of the survey's work for the future consultation.

In general, survey is a science that accurately determines the shape, area (size) and positions of a sites surface by the measurements of certain points. Surveying includes the measurements of direction and relationships of angles by the use of the surveying instruments.

The purpose of the surface exploration or survey are as following :

1. To Locate the sites.
2. To establish the site boundaries.
3. To completely plot the area.
4. To describe the topographic nature of the site.
5. To prepare a map including the site and the surrounding area including find spot in the area.

All these aspects of survey are of the utmost importance in the interpretation of the site and for the writing of its description.

OBJECTIVE OF PRESENT SURVEY

The present author has taken the exploration of Somakoi river valley which is a tributary of Brahmani, around Telkoi area in general and from Nuagarh to Danduamunda in particular. The emphasis was to locate sites basically of Holocene epoch in general and neolithic culture in particular, and also to compare the materials with other central Odishan and surraending areas of Odisha's sites.

TELKOI AND ITS LOCALITIES

Telkoi is a block of Keonjhar sub-division, situated to the southern direction and at a distance of 10 km. from Jagamohanpur Chhak (square). The village is located on the right bank of river Somakoi. This is located between 21° 22' N. latitude and 85° 24' E. longitude.

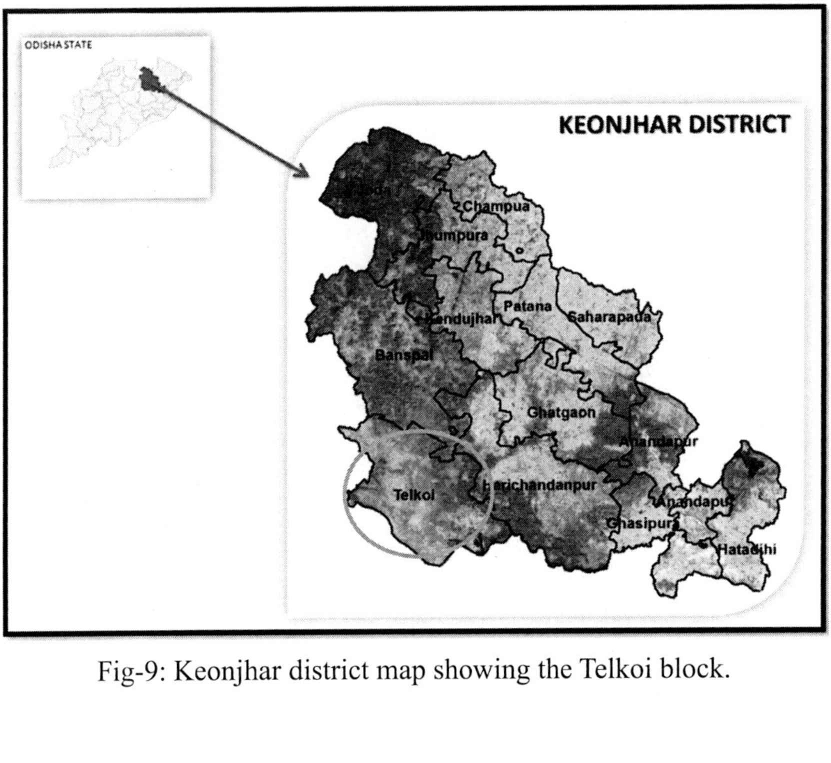

Fig-9: Keonjhar district map showing the Telkoi block.

The present exploration conducted around Telkoi, had resulted 12 prehistoric sites and one historical site within 7 Sq.km. area. The prehistoric sites are discussed in the present chapter and the historical site is discussed in the chapter of Site and excavation. All the 12 sites are divided into four units on the basis of clock-wise on Topo map. These sites are located both on foot hill area as well as in river valley i.e.

Unit-I No site has been discovered.

Unit-II Katarapali, Balisahi, Tungur Pahar, KadaliKund and Danduamunda.

Unit-III Madhusudanpur locality-1, Madhusudanpur locality-2, College Area, Madhusudanpur locality-3 and Gundurijhora.

Unit-IV Telkoi (excavated site) and Nuagarh.

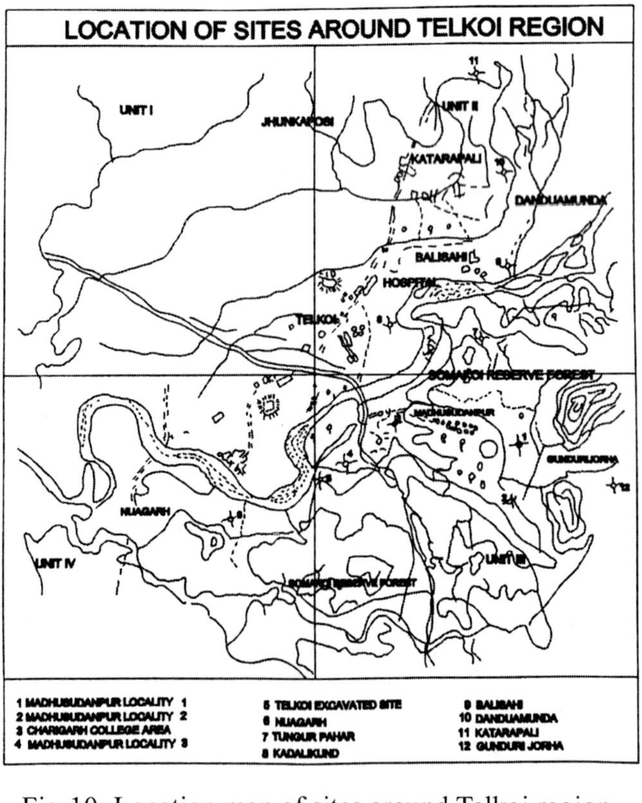

Fig-10: Location map of sites around Telkoi region.

Out of 12 sites, 8 sites are identified on the left bank and 4 sites are on the right bank. At present, the area is populated with both the tribals and non tribal groups. The tribal group includes Juang, Munda, Bhuiyan etc. The non-tribal group includes Chasa, Patra, Jhara, Gauda, Teli etc.

METHODS OF SURVEY

Any type of work needs certain methods, because without adequate methodology the work cannot be done properly. Hence certain methods are used in present exploration. Basically three methods are used for present survey. They are discussed below.

a) Intensive Exploration

This type of survey method indicates the thoroughly examination or micro study of a particular area. In this method, we have to fix up an imaginary boundary line of the area properly and systematically. By applying this method we explored the sites around Telkoi.

b) Locational method

In this method we have to locate the sites in different localities i.e. different micro eco-zones include forest, river bank, foot hill or valley, agricultural land etc.

c) Grid Method

Total 12 sites are surveyed on the Somakoi basin around Telkoi. All the sites are explored with intensive exploration method and Locational method but the Telkoi site is most concentrated and least disturbed sites among all other sites. So present author has decided to make a small scale trial excavation, first one to lay the grid on the land over where excavation is to be made. Hence, decided to layout the grid in the Telkoi.

The grid is a network of two sets of parallel lines, each of the sets survey intersecting the other at right angles. The grid survey is undertaken (i) To furnish data for making the site plan, (ii) For the purpose of orientation of a site (iii) To provide a basic reference for contours and other topographic features. The grid consists of a datum line (an imaginary line, which measured in north-south direction and in a fixed line of reference), base line (the east-west line is known as the site base line), and datum point (it is a permanently fixed point on the site that serves as a reference point for all measurements). With the help of these points, the surveyor must decide the orientation of grid its real extend and its scale. The grid should be oriented to true north and each of its intersection should be marked with a permanent stake labelled with its bearing. The size of the site will direct the scale of the grid.

LAYOUT OF GRID AT TELKOI

Before the excavation it is necessary to layout grid in a site. After the general surface survey of the area it was decided to take a small scale excavation at Telkoi. However, present author took the grid 5 x 5m. Then the whole grid was divided into 25 small grid units consists of 1 x 1 sq.m. The horizontal axis of the grid is numbered as A, B, C, D, E and the vertical axis is numbered numerically like, 1,2,3,4 and 5. After dividing the overall grid in 25 grid unit artefacts and associated materials are plotted in a graph sheet and after plotting the materials are collected. Some grid units are implementiferous and some are non-implementiferous. Hence, artefacts are not recovered in every grid units.The recoveries from the grid are both lithic and ceramic objects, the findings are analysed further in details in the script.

LOCATION OF SITES AND MATERIAL RECOVERIES

To trace out the stone age industry and know the occurrence of palaeo-relices, the study of the chrono-stratigraphy is important. Telkoi area an intensive exploration has been conducted. These explored sites reveal more or less occurrence of the lithic implements because of exposed, unexposed and highly eroded surfaces. Along with the lithic implements some ceramic objects are also recovered.

However, from the surface total 544 lithic implements and potsherds are found. There are 24 of Lower Paleolithic period, 11 of Upper Palaeolithic, 287 Microliths of Mesolithic period and 222 of Neolithic period. The recovered materials around Telkoi area have been analysed in later according to their cultural typology and technology.

Descriptions of sites are described in details in below with materials recovered from the sites.

1. MADHUSUDANPUR LOCALITY- 1 (MP-I)
(21° 21' 2" N - latitude, 85°25' E - longitude)

The site of Madhusudanpur locality-1 is located about 2.5 km east of Telkoi town near Madhusudanpur Residential Primary School along the banks of Kuamundanalla on the foot plains of Mahadev Hills. The site is an eroded area approximately of 500 x 500 m. and covered with agricultural and dense forest lands. Some recent plantation has been made on the north of the village Madhusudanpur. The site is covered with different floras like Sal *(Shorea rubusta),* Kendu *(Disopyrous emoroplerix),* Mahula *(Mudhuca longifolia),* Amla *(Phyllanthus amalice) etc.*

The artefact collected from the surface includes 4 Lower Palaeolithic tools, 3 Mesolithic and 4 Neolithic tools. The Lower Palaeolithic tools consists of hand axe and cleaver, Mesolithic are scraper and fluted core, and Neoliths are axe and blank. No soil samples are collected and no section was taken at the site.

2. MADHUSUDANPUR LOCALITY – 2 (MP-II)
(21°21' N - latitude, 85°25' E -longitude)

The site is located about 1 km. south east of the Madhusudanpur Residential primary school in the Gundurijhora revenue village area. It lies on the south of Sagatala hillock. It extends in an area measuring 200 × 100 m. on the foot plains of the hillock. The site distributed in both in the densely forest and agricultural lands of the area. The Chasa, Munda, Patra, and Bhuiyan people are local inhabitant in the area. Flora includes mainly Sal (Shorea Robusta) in this site.

From this site 11 Microliths and 6 Neoliths are found. Mesoliths implements include fluted core, scraper, blade, flake and Neoliths artefacts include 2 flake and 2 blank and 2 axe. Soil samples are collected from this site. The soil varies in colour ranging from reddish to yellowish, where as no section was taken at the site.

3. COLLEGE AREA (CA)
(21°21' 15" N - latitude, 85°23'25" E - longitude)

The site is located about 1 km east of Telkoi town along the Telkoi Gundurijorha village Road. It is an elevated rocky broken land with a small mound approximately of 400 x 300 m. of the left of Somakoi river, on which the Charigarh college is situated. The whole area has been segmented by the village road into two parts. However, the site in general has yielded a good number of microliths and Neoliths. But the elevated mound in particular presents numerous microliths. The associated finding with the typology reveals that the site was a primary manufacturing site.

From this site 2 Palaeoliths, 114 mircoliths and 36 Neoliths are recovered. Microliths include fluted core, borer, awl, flake, scraper, point, blade, burin etc. and Neolithic include axe, chisel, ring stone, hammer stone, rubber stone, blank and flakes. No section is taken where as some soil samples are collected for study purpose.

4. MADHUSUDANPUR LOCALITY - 3 (MP-III)
(21"21'3" N-latitude, 85"24'7" E-longitude)

The site is located on highly eroded rocky lands on the right of Dandsanali a perennial stream flows from the Somakoi Reserve Forests. Moreover it is located 150 m. east of Telkoi-Kaliahata Road and 250 m. to the west on the left bank of river Somakoi. A quartzite outcrop measuring 20 x 25 m. is plotted on the exposed laterite patch in the north west of the site. The site extends in an area of about 200 x 200 m. It is dotted with a deep gully runs from east to the west and some high bulk of undisturbed greyish clay silt deposit to upper reddish silt deposits. The bulks are ranging from 1 m. to 2 m. in the height. These bulks demonstrate some living old roots of Sal plants with small stumps. This proves that the site was previously covered with a dense Sal forest and now has been eroded upto lateritic gravel deposits due to geo-climatic and cultural influences to it.

From this site 1 Lower Palaeolithic, 11 Upper Palaeolithic, 57 microliths of Mesolithic and 37 Neolithic artefacts are found. The major typologies of microliths is fluted core, scraper, blade, point, flake etc. No section is taken and no soil samples are collected from this site.

5. TUNGUR PAHAR (TP)
(21°22' N-latitude, 85°25' E longitude)

Tungur Pahar a down hillock located at North of Madhusudanpur village on the left bank of river Somakoi. The site is located in the dense forest on the north of the hillock at an eroded land mass which slopes down to Kuamundanalla, a band of quartzite is exposed and stretched north-south in the site. The site has yielded various lithic artefacts from the disturbed and undisturbed surface.

From this site 2 Lower Palaeoliths, 21 microliths and 18 Neoliths are collected. The microlithic artefacts from the site include fluted core, blade, flake and borer. No stratigraphic and soil sample was collected from this site.

6. KADALI KUND (KK)
(21 °22' N-latitude, 85°24' E-longitude)

The site is located on the right bank of the river Somakoi near Veterinary Hospital. The site extends an area approximately measuring 100 x 500 m. along the left banks of the river Somakoi from Inspection Banglow to Veterinary Hospital. The Western part of the site from the bank of the river is covered with undulated agricultural lands. Near this Kadali Kunda bathing ghat number of Palaeolithic tools have been collected from the sand deposit as well as on the agricultural lands. Some Neoliths are also collected from the elevated barren land. The Iron slags are also distributed on a mound very close to the river. Moreover, on the left bank of the river Somakoi a section has been studied on a straight cut terrace. A lense of stratigraphy was recorded from mottled clay to (humus) recent deposits. The lower pebble gravel and upper pebble gravels of this section yielded pebble tools like chopper, hand axes and the upper pebble gravel yielded large flake tools as well.

From this site 11 Lower Paleolithic tools are found, such as chopper, cleaver and hand axe. 5 Neoliths are also recovered from this site.

7. BALISAHI (BS)
(21°22' N-latitude, 85°25' E-longitude)

It is barren land approximately 300 x150 m. located at the confluence of Baghamundanalla and on the right bank of the river Somakoi to the east of the village Balisahi. The site has got much erosional slopes and terraces all round the elevated patch. A high voltage powerline tower is erected on this land. South of this patch has recently been converted to agricultural land by the local people. The site has been exposed due to heavy erosion of soil and formed small rain gully and cliff on patches. At a place to the east on the right bank of Bhagamundanalla a cliff has been exposed and yielded bar axes of high workmanship in a clear cut stratigraphic position. The Munda and Bhuiyan ethnic people are inhabited in the village.

From this site 68 microliths of Mesolithic and 19 Neoliths artefacts are found. The important artefacts collected from the site are fluted core, scraper, blade, flake, borer, point and notch. One section and soil sample is taken for stratigraphical study.

8. DANDUAMUNDA (DM)
(21°22'25" N-latitude, 85°25'10" E-longitude)

The site is located west of the village Danduamunda at a little depressed area near by agricultural lands. The site extends in an area approximately 100 x 50 m. The village has been inhabited by ethnic groups like Gond, Jhora (Gold Collector), and Lohar (Black Smith). So an ethno-archaeological study on Jhora people has been made in terms of their traditional gold collection from river gravels.

From this site two Neolithic artefacts are found. Soil samples are are taken to understand the geo-morphology of the area.

9. KATRAPALI (KP)
(21°23' N-latitude, 85°25' E-longitude)

The site is surrounded by a densely forest hillock to the north of the Katrapali village. It is located 1.5 kms. north of Katrapali on the east of the old N.H.6 from Keonjhar to Telkoi. This is an open air area site and least disturbed. The ethnic group Munda, Ho and Bhuiyan are inhabited in the village.

From this site five neoliths are found. No soil samples was collected from the site whereas one section was taken for study the stratigraphy.

10. TELKOI (TK)
(21°22' N- latitude, 85°24' E-longitude)

The site is located on the left bank of Somakoi river in agricultural land parallel to the northern boundary of Somakoi Reserve Forest, open Sal Jungle to the south of the site. A perennial stream `Dandsanali' flows very close to the north of the site which meets the river Somakoi in the north-west of the site. Trial excavation work conducted in this site has resulted in discovery of neolithic flakes and chips associated with ceramic remains from different levels. The south and east portion of the site is relatively undisturbed whereas the extreme north-west of the site is highly disturbed and eroded down to the river Somakoi.

The site is an open air site. From this site 2 Lower Palaeolithic tools, 8 Microliths and 85 Neolithic implements are recovered from surface outside the grid. From the grid 61 lithic artefacts and 44 potsherds are also recovered. The microliths comprised of scraper, fluted core, flake, blade etc. and Neoliths is comprising of axe. The recovered potsherds from grid are mainly of red ware.

11. NUAGARH (NG)
(21°21' N-latitude, 85°23'30"E-longitude)

The site is located in a dense scrub of Somakoi R.F. at the right bank of river Somakoi. It is situated lies on the northern foot hills of an unknown hillock near the village Nuagarh. The village Nuagarh is situated 1.5 km. of the site on the left bank of river Somakoi. The site is a rocky elevated land distributed in the cobbles of quartzite and sand stone.

From this site 2 Lower Palaeolithic, 5 Mesolithic, and 4 Neolithic artefacts are found. Microliths include fluted core, scraper, blade etc. One section was taken at the site. The soil sample taken from this site varies in colour ranging from reddish to yellowish.

Danduamunda site

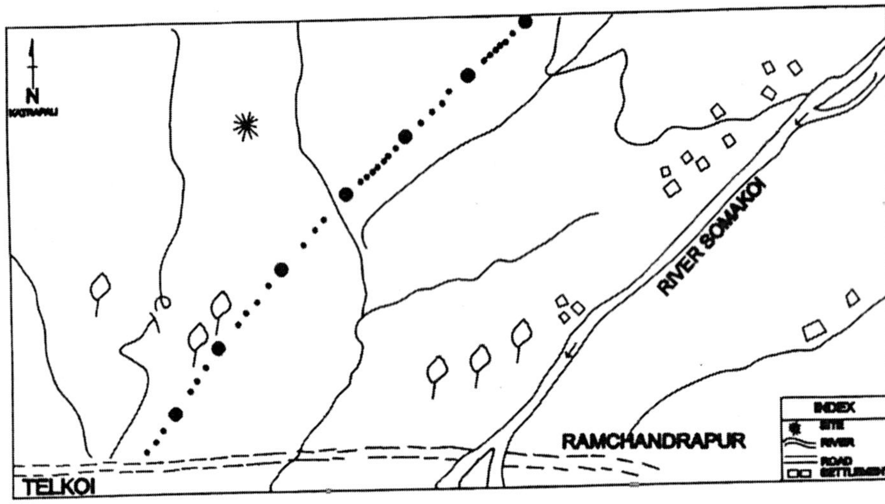

Nuagarh site

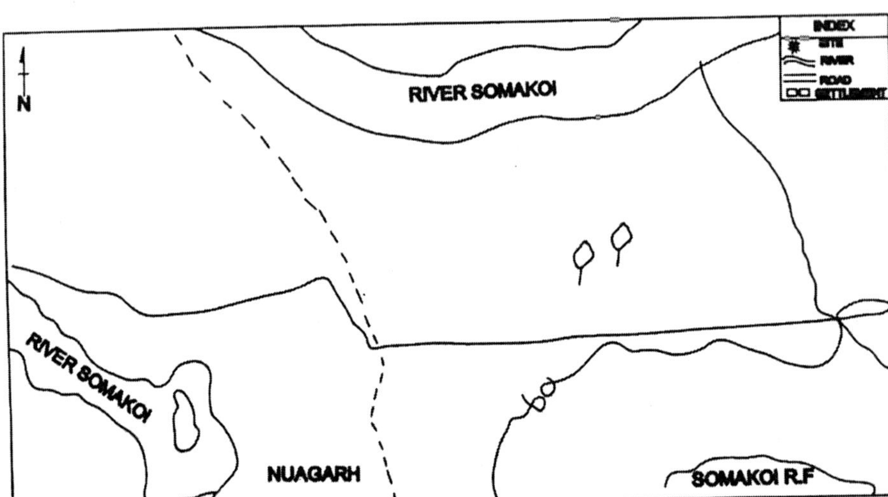

Fig-11: Topo map showing Danduamunda and Nuagarh site.

Telkol site

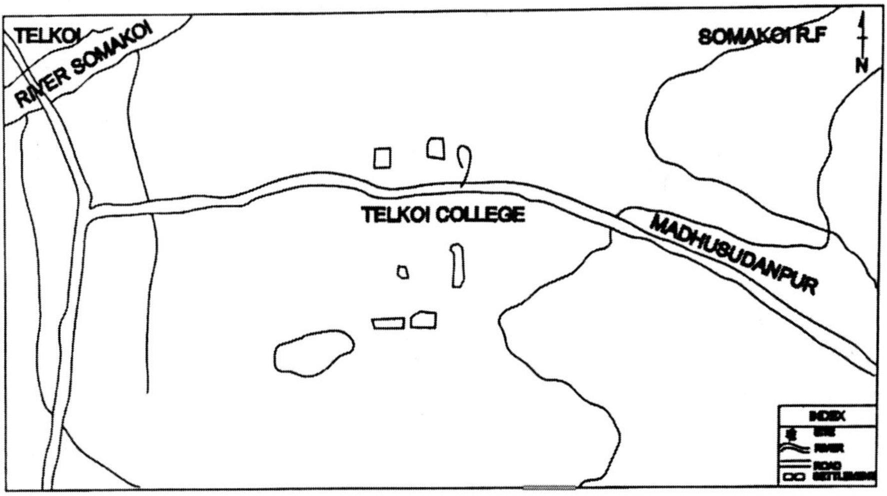

Tungur pahar site

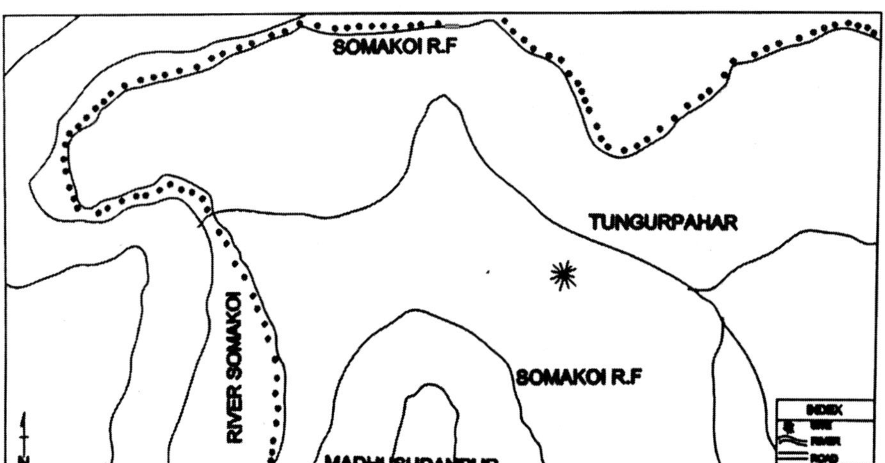

Fig-12: Topo map showing Telkoi and Tungur Pahar site.

Kadalikund site

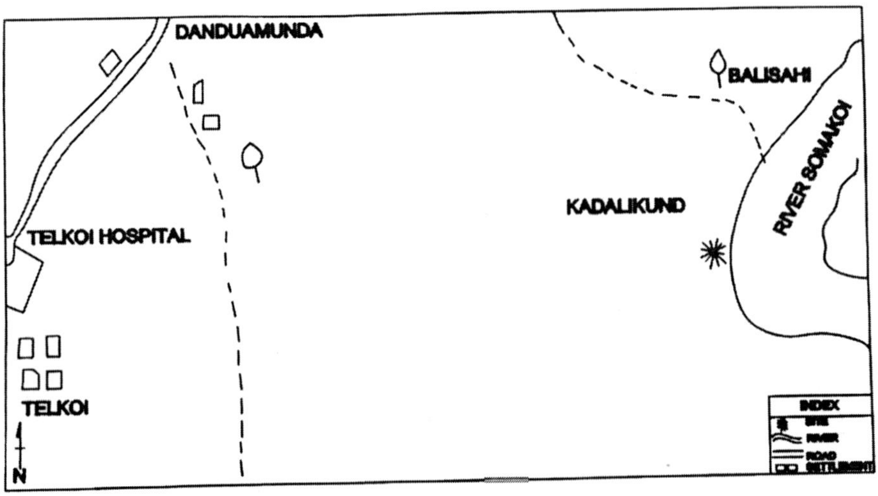

Balisahi site

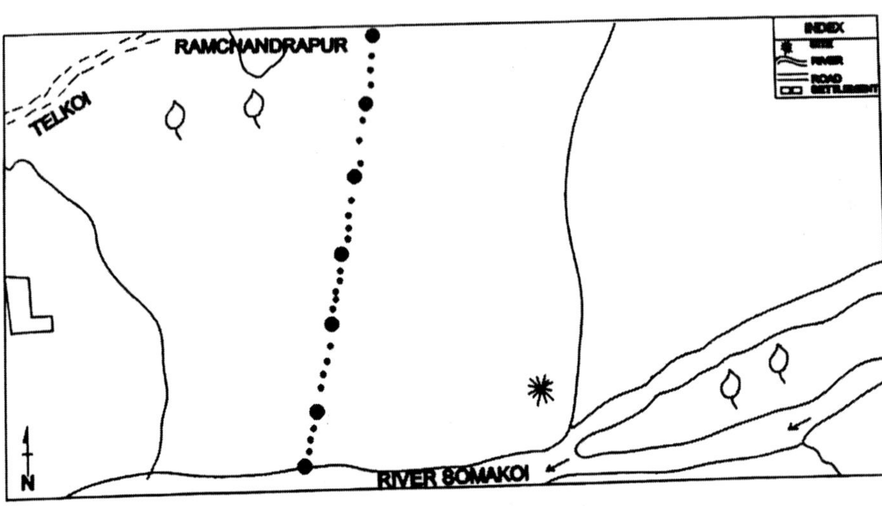

Fig- 13: Topo map showing Kadalikund and Balisahi site.

Gundurijhora site

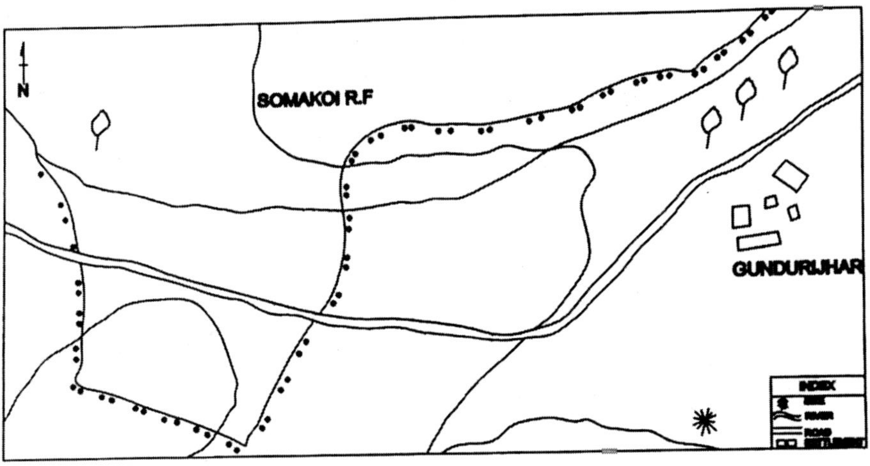

Katrapali site

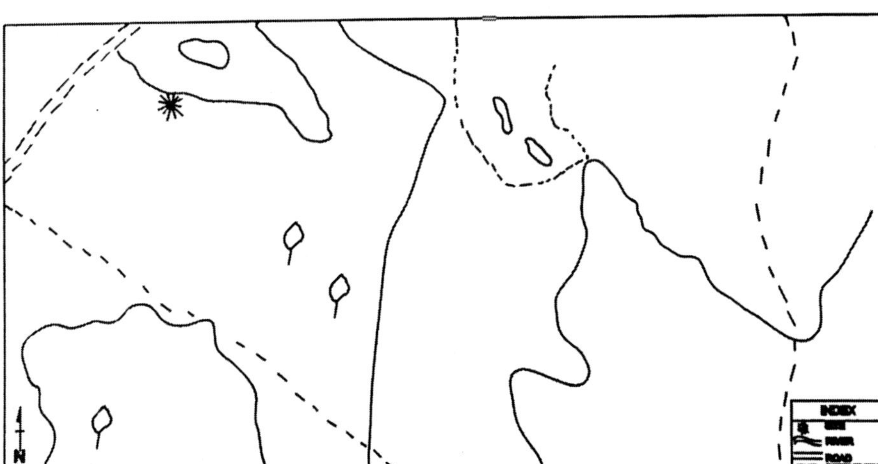

Fig-14: Topo map showing Gundurijhora and Katarapali site.

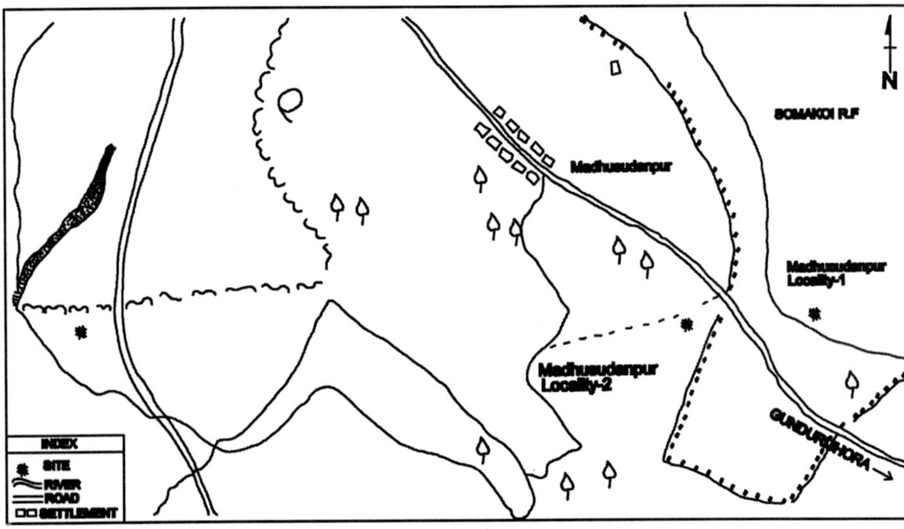

Fig-15: Topo Map showing Madhusudanpur locality-1,2 and 3 site

12. GUNDURIJHORA (GJ)
(21°21' N-latitude, 85°25' 30" E-longitude)

The site is located on the valley of Kuamunda Hills and Mahadev Hills. It is a narrow depressed plain land with reddish brown soil. This area has been inhabited by Pauri Bhuiyan and Juang. The area shows source of quartzite and quartz rocks. From this site, only one Neoliths tool is found.

Unit - 1 UN-EXPLORED

The Unit-1 of the study area has not been studied due to its topography. The area has densely forest land with some wild furiously animals like bear and hyena. The landscape is not easy to access which covered with dense forest and agricultural lands with thickly grass lands. Due to this topographic feature the present pre-historic research on that particular segment is not made and no site of archaeological content has been recorded.

With this background, it is important to discusss stratigraphy, physical and chemical analysis of soil, site-wise and type-wise distribution of lithic components, average metric measurement of lithic component, description and drawing of artefacts are the theme of the next chapter.

CHAPTER 3

DATA ANALYSIS

STRATIGRAPHY

The study of stratigraphy in prehistoric archaeology is one of the most important aspects of exploration and excavation. Through the recognition of stratigraphic difference between sites, the sequential cultural history of an area is derived and chrono-stratigraphy is established. Stratigraphy is the study of strata or the different layers and levels of occupation on an archaeological site and their relation to each other and the determination of the cultural sequence which they were laid down. Hence, during the surface exploration a special attempt was paid to study the stratigraphy of the area as for as possible.

The purpose of stratigraphy is to understand geochronological aspect of the culture. Hence, an attempt has been made in Telkoi region. Sections are exposed along the banks of rivers and streams. In the present exploration three sections are taken for the study of stratigraphy of this region.

Table 1: Distribution of Sections at Telkoi study area

Name of Site	Section taken
Madhusudanpur locality-1	_
Madhusudanpur locality-2	_
Madhusudanpur locality-3	1
Balisahi	1
Kadalikund	1
Gundurijhora	_
Katarapali	_
Danduamunda	_
Telkoi	_
Tungur Pahar	_
College Area	_
Nuagarh	_

Three sections are taken from 12 explored sites around Telkoi area. In Kadalikund and Balisahi the section ware taken in the left bank of river Somakoi and in Madhusudanpur locality-3 site, thc section was taken from a bank of local stream called Dandasanali.

Table 2: Section at Kadalikunda

Drainage	Depositions	Height (m)	Implementiferous Strata	Remarks
Somakoi	Humus	0.6	Nil	8 Soil
	Red silt	2.40	,,	Samples
	Coarse sand	1.10	,,	are collected
	Reddish silty clay	0.52	,,	
	Brownish silty clay	0.62	,,	
	Upper pebble gravel	0.45	Yes	
	Coarse sand	0.42	Nil	
	Lower pebble gravel	1.10	Yes	
	TOTAL	6.67m		

Table showing the distribution of stratigraphy in Kadalikund.

Table 3: Section at Balisahi

Drainage	Depositions	Height (m)	Implimentiferous Strata	Remarks
Somakoi near Balisahi	Brown silty clay	0.45	Yes	3 Soil Samples are collected
	Yellowish brown clay	1.30	,,	
	Greyish brown Clay	0.80	,,	
	TOTAL	2.55m		

Table showing the distribution of stratigraphy in Balisahi Section.

Table 4: Section at Madhusudanpur locality- 3

Drainage	Depositions	Height (m)	Implimentiferous Strata	Remarks
Dandasanali	Red silt	2.30	Yes	3 Soil Samples are collected
	Coarse fine sand	2.50	Nil	
	Loose Lateritic	4.50	,,	
	Bed rock		,,	
	TOTAL	9.30m		

Table showing the distribution of stratigraphy in Madhusudanpur locality-3 section.

The above table shows the depositions and their heights. The height of the section at Kadalikund is 6.67m, the height of Madhusudanpur locality-3 section is 9.30m. and the height of Balisahi section is 2.55m. The nature of stratigraphic depositions was studied around the locality with the help of three sections. One section was pooled from a local stream near village and other sections were studied from the river Somakoi.

Regarding the deposition, the section at Kadalikund has revealed the deposition of humus, upper loose gravel, upper pebble, coarse silty gravel and lower pebble measuring the height of 6.67m. The Section at Madhusudanpur locality-3 reveals the depositions of red silt, coarse fine sand, loose laterite and lateritic bed rock measuring the height 9.30m. Here humus deposition is not found because the surface is highly eroded in this site. The section at Balisahi deposits are brown silt, yellowish brown clay and greyish brown clay and measuring 2.55 m.

Analysing these three sections and their depositions, it is found that the stratigraphy of local stream and Somakoi river bank are not similar. But briefly the pattern of deposition can be segmented into two types, such as gravel and silt.

SOIL: PHYSICAL AND CHEMICAL ANALYSIS

Analysing of soil is an important aspect in archaeology to date sites and to know something about the environment at the time of formation. In most instances from natural or manmade deposition, the pedologist can distinguish among water laid, wind laid and man laid deposits.

Physical features of soil include the particle size, particle shape, grain surface and colour.

(a) Particle Size

The composition of a sediment in terms of its texture is important due to its origin. For example, gravels tend to be derived from rapid river flow or strong wave action. There are several schemes of classification here the British system is varying percentage of clay, silt and sand are used to give precision to soil description such as silty clay.

(b) Particle Shape

The two main shapes are rounded and angular. Intermediate shape are known as sub-rounded and sub-angular. Rounded particle indicate a substantial period of transport and angular particles indicate little or no transport.

(C) Grain Surface

Clay	-	0.002 mm. or less
Silt	-	0.002 mm.0.06 mm
Sand	-	0.06 mm 2.0 mm
Gravel (pebble)	-	2.0 mm 60.0 mm
Stone (Cobble)	-	60.0 mm and over

Features of the surface of sand grains can indicate whether the material is of wind-blown or aquatic origin.

(d) Colour of Soil

Colour is useful to guide humus and iron content. Dark-brown, greys or black usually indicate high humus content, and thus an old top soil. A pale colour indicates either rapid deposition of sediments or teaching in a soil. Orange and red colours indicate high iron content-colour is usually defined by matching the soil sample with a standard, a Munsell colour chart being the most widely used set of standards. It is important that standard colours are used in soil and sediments description to enable comparison to be made from site to site.

Table 5: Physical Analysis of Soil Sample, Madhusudanpur locality-3

Soil Sample	Colour	Consolidated	Unconsolidated
Layer-1	Reddish brown	Wet	dry
Layer-2	Gray	,,	,,
Layer-3	Yellowish brown	,,	,,
Layer-4	Yellowish	,,	,,

In the above table it is analysed that colour of the soil are different in each layer. The soil sample numbers are given on the basis of layer. The soil samples also are tested on the basis of consolidation condition. If the soil is breakable in nature then it is called as unconsolidated and if it is unbreakable then known as consolidated. This is identified in both dry and wet condition of the soil. The colour of the soil are reddish brown, grey, yellowish brown and yellowish.

Table 6: Physical Analysis of Soil Sample, Kadalikund

Soil Sample	Colour	Consolidated	Unconsolidated
Layer-1	Yellowish brown	Wet	dry
Layer-2	Gray	,,	,,
Layer-3	Reddish brown	,,	,,
Layer-4	Reddish	,,	,,

In the above table the colour is ranging between yellow brown to reddish.

SIEVE ANALYSIS

The objective of the sieve analysis is to know the content of different soil types present in the soil samples. For this purpose three sieves are used namely 2 mm, 0.02 mm and 0.06 mm. 10 gm of soil were analysed using the above mention sieves and the residue have been measured to identify the soil type. The residue of 2 mm sieve has been contains as coarse sand or gravel, residue of 0.02 mm. sieve has been fine sand. The purpose of expression of percentage is to identify the significance of soil.

Table 7: Sieve Analysis of Soil sample from Madhusudanpur locality-3

Section at Site	Soil sample	Layer	Sieve Size				Remarks
			2 mm	0.2 mm	0.06 mm	Residue	
Madhusudanpur locality-3	1	1	1gm	1gm	1gm	7gm	10% coarse sand, 10% fine sand,10% silt & 70% clay
	2	2	2.5gm	1gm	0.5gm	6gm	25% coarse sand, 10% find sand, 5% silt & 60% clay
	3	3	2gm	1gm	1gm	6gm	20% coarse sand, 10% find sand, 10% silt & 60% clay
	4	4	0gm	2.5gm	0.5gm	7gm	0% coarse sand, 25% find sand, 5% silt & 70% clay

Table 8: Sieve Analysis of Soil from Kadalikund

Section at Site	Soil Sample	Layer	Sieve Size				Remarks
			2 mm	0.2 mm	0.06 mm	Residue	
Kadali Kund	1	1	0.5gm	1gm	1.5gm	7gm	5% coarse sand, 10% fine sand, 15% silt & 70% clay.
	2	2	2gm	1gm	1gm	6gm	20% coarse sand, 10% find sand, 5% silt & 60% clay.
	3	3	1.5gm	1gm	0.5gm	7gm	15% coarse sand, 10% fine sand, 5% silt & 70% clay.
	4	4	0gm	2gm	1gm	7gm	0% coarse sand 20% find sand, 10% silt & 70% clay.
	5	5	0gm	1gm	1gm	8gm	0% coarse sand 10% fine sand, 10% silt & 80% clay.

CHEMICAL ANALYSIS OF THE SOIL

The chemical reaction of a soil sample frequently determines the sort of changes which can take place in it and generally desirable to know the outset of any chemical examination. PH (Hydrogen-Ion) is a measure of the absolute degree of acidic or alkalinity of soil.

In practice the PH scale ranges from 0 to 14, the range found in moist-temperate soils varying between 4.0 (very acidic) to something over 9.0 (strongly alkaline), the majority given values between 5.5 and 8.5.

Various methods exist for the measurement of PH values. One method has taken into consideration for the present purpose i.e. Colorimetric method using the BDA (Universal indicator).

Method:

First take the soil in a capillary tube and add a little amount of distilled water and centrifuge. After this some transparent water comes over the soil and we have to collect that water in another capillary tube. After adding the KCL solution to this transparent water the universal indicator (BDH)1 is added. By this method one can know the acidic and alkalinity contents of the soil.

Drawback of the method are the time consumed in testing considerable numbers of sample adding to the constant washing upland rinsing with distilled water of the tiny glasses and capillaries. Without this care no degree of accuracy can be assured.

The acid test was applied to note the acidity and alkalinity of the soil 20% HCL (Hydrochloric acid) was taken for the purpose of test. The test may indicate high, medium, low and no reaction.

Table 9: Chemical Analysis of Soil, Madhusudanpur locality-3

Section at site	Soil sample	layer	HCL				PH	
			Nil	High	Medium	Low	Colour	No
Madhusundanpur locality-3	1	1		-			Neutral 7.0	CH2
	2	2		-			Strongly acidic 5.0	CH2
	3	3		-			Neutral 7.0	CH2
	4	4		-			Slightly acidic 6.0	CH1

According to the above table no reaction is found from 4 soil sample of Madhusudanpur locality-3. By PH test it is decided that out of 4 samples 2 are neutral, one is strongly acidic and one is slightly acidic.

Table 10: Chemical Analysis of Soil, Kadalikund

Section at site	Soil sample	layer	HCL				PH	
			Nil	High	Medium	Low	Colour	No
Kadali Kund	1	1		-			Neutral 7.0	CH2
	2	2		-			Neutral 7.0	CH2
	3	3		-			Strongly acidic 5.0	CH2
	4	4		-			Slightly acidic 6.0	CH2
	5	5		-			Slightly acidic 6.0	CH1

According to the above table no reaction is found from 5 soil samples of Kadalikund. By PH test it is decided that out of 5 samples 2 are neutral, one is strongly acidic, two are slightly acidic.

CULTURAL SEGMENTS (SURFACE)

By intensive surface exploration 12 sites has been discovered. All the surveyed sites except Gundurijhora were implementiferous. A few palaeolithic tools have been collected from Kadalikund, Madhusudanpur locality-1, College area, Madhusudanpur locality-3, and Tungur Pahar. Mostly microliths and ground stones of neolithic period have been collected from the whole area. The cultural period may be classified into four different cultural phase, such as, Lower Palaeolithic, Upper Palaeolithic, Mesolithic and Neolithic.

(a) Lower Palaeolithic

On the typo-technological evolutionary sequences the lower palaeolithic period is known as first cultural phase. The characteristic tool types of this period are known as hand axe, chopper, cleaver etc. In the present survey lower palaeolithic tools have been recovered from seven sites such as Madhusudanpur locality-1, College area, Madhusudanpur locality-3, Tungur pahar, Nuagarh, Telkoi and Kadalikund. From these seven sites 24 Palaeolithic tools are found. Out of 24 implements there are 4 choppers, 12 hand axes, 4 cleavers and 4 flakes of Lower Palaeolithic period.

(b) Upper Palaeolithic

From Madhusudanpur locality-3 upper palaeolithic implements are recovered. These implements are mainly flake, blades and scraper. This is the only site from which author recovered Upper Palaeolithic implements.

(c) Mesolithic

Mesolithic period is transitional one between palaeolithic and neolithic during the early part of Holocene period. The characteristic tool type of this period is known by the term microliths and they can be classified according to their shape and size, from the present exploration, out of 12 surveyed sites 8 are evidenced microliths.

(d) Neolithic

In the cultural history of human being neolithic age is associated with farming and cultivating using these stone implement. The cultural period being the concluding phase of lithic culture is marked by more evolved and developed typo-technological features. The characteristic feature of neolithic age is the grinding and polishing stone tools. From the present exploration the Neolithic typologies includes axe, adze, chisel and ring stone.

Table 11: Site wise Distribution of Lithic Tools (Excluding Telkoi Trial Excavation)

Name of the site	Lower Palaeolithic	Upper Palaeolithic	Mesolithic	Neolithic	Total No
Madhusudanpur locality-1	4	-	3	4	11
Madhusudanpur locality-2	-	-	11	6	17
Madhusudanpur locality-3	1	11	57	37	106
College Area	2	-	114	36	152
Tungur Pahar	2	-	21	18	41
Balisahi	-	-	68	19	87
Kadalikund	11	-	-	5	16
Danduamunda	-	-	-	2	2
Katarapali	-	-	-	5	5
Nuagarh	2	-	5	4	11
Telkoi	2	-	8	85	95
Gundurijhora	-	-	-	1	1
Total	24	11	287	222	544

The above table indicated the surface data of the 12 sites around Telkoi. The tools are recovered from the 12 sites broadly belonging to four cultural periods i.e. lower Palaeolithic, Upper palaeolithic Mesolithic and Neolithic. Total 544 tools are collected from the surface, out of which 24 are from lower palaeolithic, 11 upper palaeolithic, 287 from mesolithic and 222 from neolithic period.

Table 12: Distribution of Lower Palaeolithic

No. of site	Typology	No	Percentage
7	Hand axe	12	50%
	Chopper	4	16.66%
	Cleaver	4	16.66%
	Flake	4	16.66%
Total		24	99.98%

Table 13: Distribution of Upper Palaeolithic

No. of site	Typology	No	Percentage
1	Flake	4	36.36%
	Nodule	1	9.09%
	Blade	2	18.18%
	Scraper	4	36.36%
Total		11	99.99%

In the above table, 11 upper palaeolithic tools are found. Flake and scraper both four in number where as one nodule and two blades are reported.

Table 14: Distribution of Mesolithic

No. of site	Typology	No	Percentage
8	Fluted core	69	24.04%
	Flake	41	14.28%
	Blade	99	34.49%
	Awl	3	1.04%
	Borer	9	3.13%
	Burin	7	2.43%
	Point	17	5.92%
	Scraper	40	13.93%
	Notch	2	0.69%
Total		287	99.95%

Analysing the table, there are 287 microliths recovered from 8 different surveyed sites. Among the microliths flakes, fluted core, blade and scraper are dominant variety.

Table 15: Distribution of Neolithic

No. of site	Typology	No	Percentage
12	Chisel	9	4.05 %
	Axe	17	7.65 %
	Ring stone	34	15.31 %
	Hammer stone	9	4.05 %
	Quern	1	0.45 %

	Rubber stone	4	1.80 %
	Cobble	2	0.90 %
	Chips	42	18.91 %
	Polisher	4	1.80 %
	Blank	15	6.75 %
	Flake	85	38.28 %
Total		222	99.95 %

Analysing the table, from 12 explored site total 222 neoliths is found. Flakes and ring stone are the dominant types. Here the number of materials and their percentage are given.

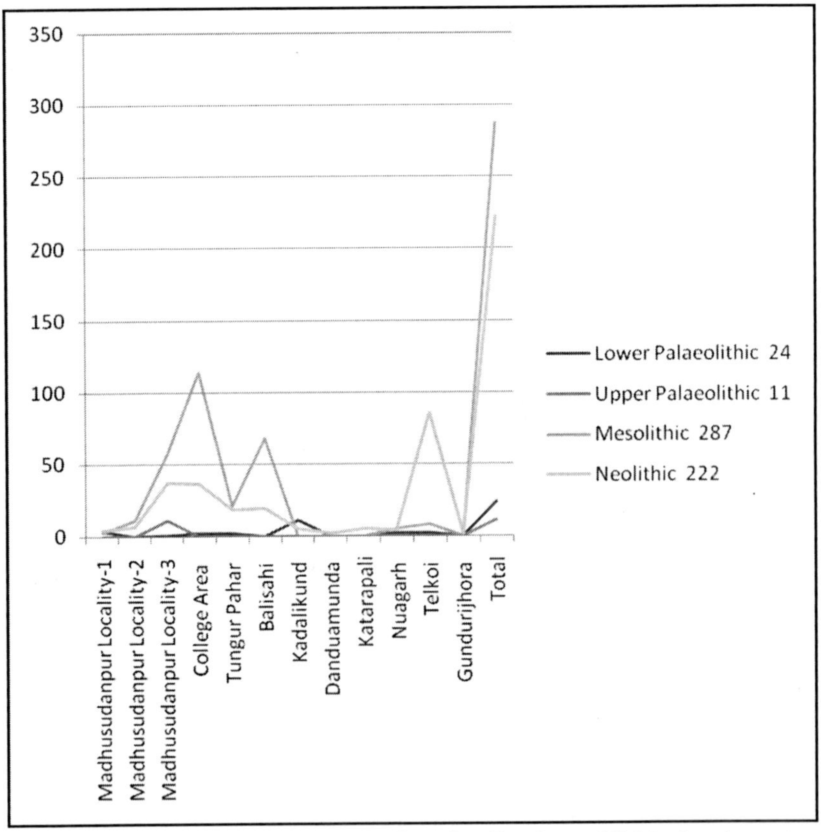

Fig-16: Chart representing site-wise distribution of lithic implements

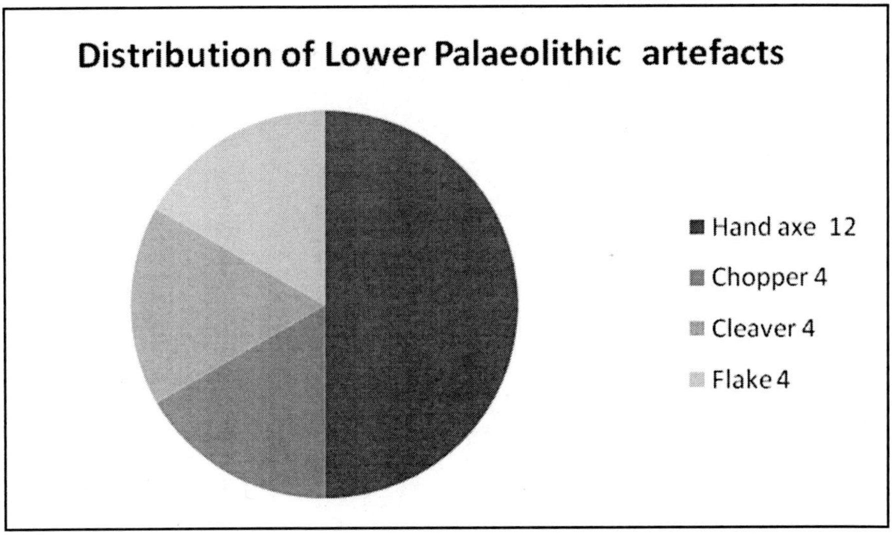

Fig-17: Pie chart representing the distribution of Lower Palaeolithic artefacts

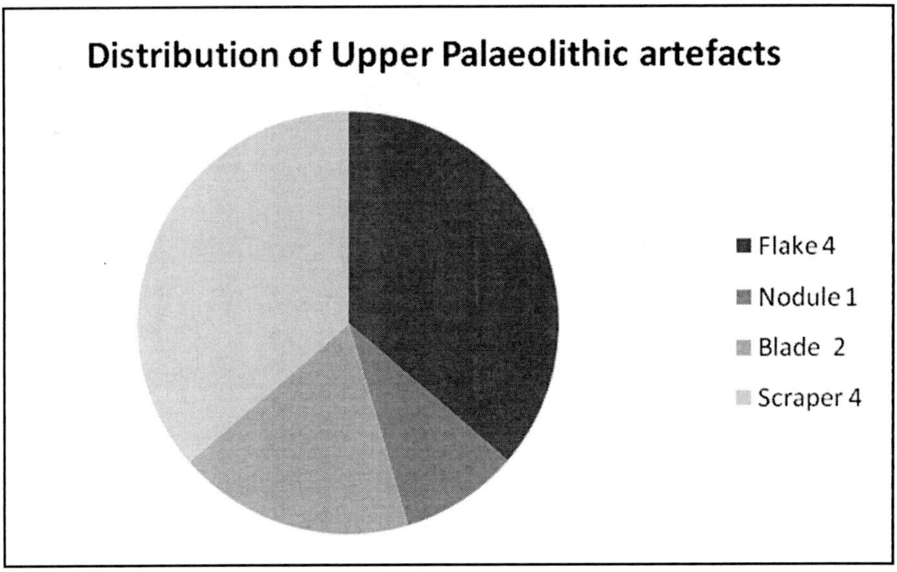

Fig-18: Pie chart representing the distribution of Upper Palaeolithic artefacts

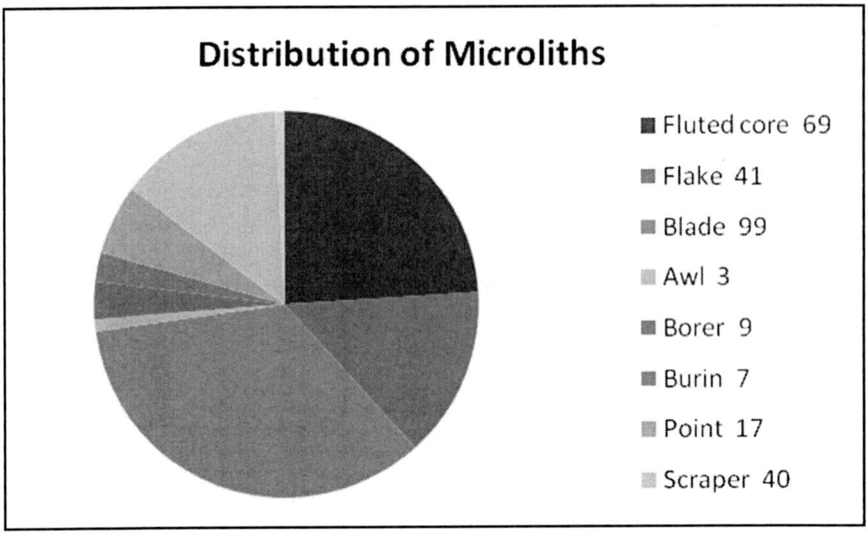

Fig-19: Pie chart representing the distribution of Microliths

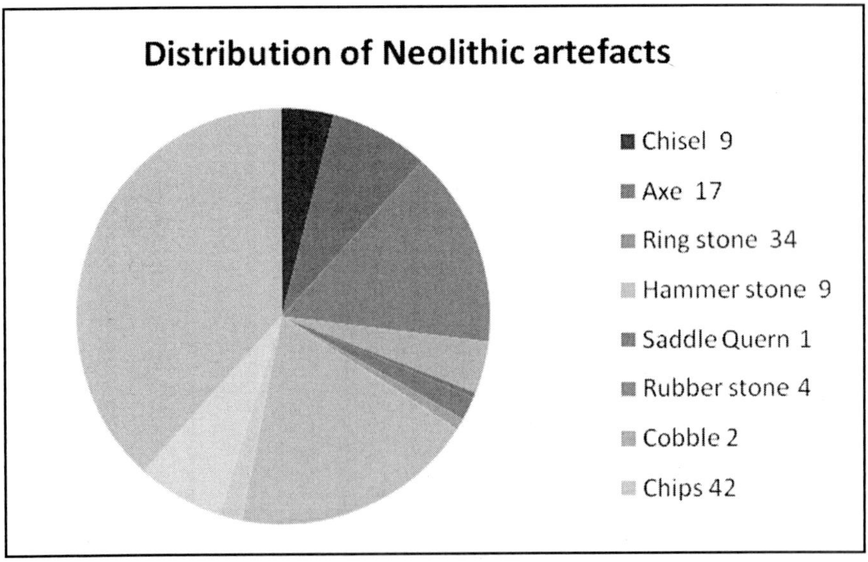

Fig-20: Pie chart representing the distribution of Neoliths

Table 16: Type-wise distribution of Lower Palaeolithic in Madhusudanpur locality-1

Name of site	Typology	No	Percentage
Madhusudanpur locality 1	Hand axe	3	75%
	Cleaver	1	25%
Total		4	100%

The above table shows that from Madhusudanpur Locality-1 site three hand axe and one cleaver of lower Palaeolithic are found.

Table 17: Type-wise distribution of Lower Palaeolithic in College Area

Name of site	Typology	No	Percentage
College area	Hand axe	1	50%
	Chopper	1	50%
Total		2	100%

The above table shows that from College area site one chopper and one hand axes of lower Palaeolithic period are found.

Table 18: Type-wise distribution of Lower Palaeolithic in Madhusudanpur locality-3

Name of site	Typology	No	Percentage
Madhusudanpur Locality-3	Hand axe	1	100%
Total		1	100%

The above table shows that from Madhusudanpur locality-3 site one hand axe of lower Palaeolithic period is found.

Table 19: Type-wise distribution of Lower Palaeolithic in Tungur Pahar

Name of site	Typology	No	Percentage
Tungur Pahar	Hand axe	1	50%
	Chopper	1	50%
Total		2	100%

The given table shows lower Palaeolithic artefacts with evolutionary order in Tungur Pahar and the number and percentage of the recovered materials.

Table 20: Type-wise distribution of Lower Palaeolithic in Kadalikund

Name of site	Typology	No	Percentage
Kadalikund	Hand axe	6	54.54%
	Cleaver	3	27.27%
	Chopper	2	18.18%
Total		11	100%

Analysing the above table it is seen that there are 3 types of lower palaeolithic tool in their evolutionary order found in Kadalikund site. Total 11 lower palaeolithic tool are recovered with dominant type of hand axe.

Table 21: Type-wise distribution of Lower Palaeolithic in Telkoi

Name of the site	Typology	No	Percentage
Telkoi	Flakes	2	100%
Total		2	100%

In the above table, two lower palaeolithic flakes are found.

Table 22: Type-wise distribution of Lower palaeolithic in Nuagarh

Name of the site	Typology	No	Percentage
Nuagarh	Flakes	2	100%
Total		2	100%

In the table, two Lower Palaeolithic flake have been noticed.

Table 23:
Site-wise and typology-wise analysis of artefacts of Lower Palaeolithic

Tool Type	Madhusudanpur Locality-1	Madhusudanpur Locality-3	College Area	TungurPahar	Kadalikund	Nuagarh	Telkoi	No	Percentage
Hand Axe	3	1	1	1	6	-	-	12	50%
Chopper	-	-	1	1	2	-	-	4	16.66%
Cleaver	1	-	-	-	3	-	-	4	16.66%
Flake	-	-	-	-	-	2	2	4	16.66%
Total	4 (16.66%)	1 (4.16%)	2 (8.33%)	2 (8.33%)	11 (45.83%)	2 (8.33%)	2 (8.33%)	24	99.98%

The above table indicate the site-wise and typology–wise data of Lower Palaeolithic sites. The artefacts are recovered from seven sites belonging to four typological categories. Total 24 artefacts are collected such as 12 hand axe, 4 chopper, 4 cleaver and 4 flake.

UPPER PALAEOLITHIC:

Table 24: Type-wise distribution of Upper Palaeolithic in Madhusudanpur locality-3

Name of the site	Typology	No	Percentage
Madhusudanpur Locality-3	Flakes	4	36.36%
	Nodule	1	9.09%
	Blade	2	18.18%
	Scraper	4	36.36%
Total		11	99.99%

In the above table, 11 Upper Palaeolithic tool are recovered such as flake; 4, scraper; 4, nodule; 1 and blade; 2.

MESOLITHIC :

Table 25: Type-wise distribution of Microliths in Madhusudanpur locality-1

Name of the site	Typology	No	Percentage
Madhusudanpur locality-1	Fluted core	2	66%
	Scraper	1	33%
Total		3	99%

The given table shows the microliths of Madhusudanpur locality-1 site. Two fluted core and one scraper of microliths are found.

Table 26: Type-wise distribution of Microliths in Madhusudanpur locality-2

Name of the site	Typology	No	Percentage
Madhusudanpur locality -2	Fluted core	1	9.09%
	Scraper	4	36.36%
	Blade	2	18.18%
	Flake	4	36.36%
Total		11	99%

According to the above table, there are four types of microliths found in Madhusudanpur Locality-2. Total microliths in this site is 11 numbers. The flake and scraper are the dominant type.

Table 27: Type-wise distribution of Microliths in Madhusudanpur locality-3

Name of the site	Typology	No	Percentage
Madhusudanpur locality-3	Fluted core	23	40.35%
	Scraper	10	17.54%
	Blade	15	26.31%
	Flake	3	5.26%
	Awl	1	1.75%
	Borer	2	3.50%
	Point	3	5.26%
Total		57	99.97%

Analysing the above table it is seen that there are seven types of microliths in their evolutionary order found in Madhusudanpur locality-3 site. Total microliths are recovered with dominant type of fluted core and blade.

Table 28: Type-wise distribution of Microliths in College Area

Name of the site	Typology	No	Percentage
College area	Fluted core	21	18.42%
	Scraper	13	11.40%
	Blade	44	38.50%
	Flake	17	14.91%
	Awl	2	1.75%
	Borer	3	2.63%
	Point	7	6.14%
	Burin	7	6.14%
Total		114	99.98%

The above table shows that the distribution of microliths with their evolutionary order in College area site. Total 114 microliths are recovered with dominant type of fluted core and blade.

Table 29: Type-wise distribution of Microliths in Tungur Pahar

Name of the site	Typology	No	Percentage
Tungur Pahar	Fluted core	10	47.61%
	Blade	5	23.80%
	Flake	5	23.80%
	Borer	1	4.76%
Total		21	99.97%

Analysing the above table shows that fluted core 10, flakes 5, blades 5 and borer 1 recovered from Tungur Pahar site.

Table 30: Type-wise distribution of Microliths in Balisahi

Name of the site	Typology	No	Percentage
Balisahi	Fluted core	9	13.23%
	Scraper	6	8.82%
	Blade	31	45.58%
	Flake	10	14.70%
	Borer	3	4.41%
	Point	7	10.29%
	Notch	2	2.94%
Total		68	99.97%

The above table shows the distribution of microliths with their evolutionary order in Balisahi site. Out of 68 implements, 9 fluted core, 10 flake, 31 blade, 3 borer, 7 point, 6 scraper and 2 notch are recovered. The dominant type is blade.

Table 31: Type-wise distribution of Microliths in Nuagarh

Name of the site	Typology	No	Percentage
Nuagarh	Fluted core	1	20%
	Flake	1	20%
	Blade	1	20%
	Scraper	2	40%
Total		5	100%

Analysing the above table, it is observed that out of 5 microliths implement of Mesolithic period, fluted core 1, flake 1, blade 1 and scraper 2 are collected for detailed study.

Table 32: Type-wise distribution of Microliths in Telkoi

Name of the site	Typology	No	Percentage
Telkoi	Fluted core	2	25%
	Flake	1	12.5%
	Blade	1	12.5%
	Scraper	4	50%
Total		8	100%

The above table indicates four types microliths tools are found from Telkoi site. Total 8 tools are collected which includes fluted core 2, flake 1, blade 1 and scraper 4.

Table 33:Site-wise and typology-wise analysis of artefacts of Mesolithic

Tool Type	Madhusudanpur Locality-1	Madhusudanpur Locality-2	Madhusudanpur Locality-3	College Area	TungurPahar	Balisahi	Nuagarh	Telkoi	No	percentage
Fluted core	2	1	23	21	10	9	1	2	69	24.04%
Flake	-	4	3	17	5	10	1	1	41	14.28%
Blade	-	2	15	44	5	31	1	1	99	34.49%
Awl	-	-	1	2	-	-	-	-	3	1.04%
Borer	-	-	2	3	1	3	-	-	9	3.13%
Burin	-	-	-	7	-	-	-	-	7	2.43%
Point	-	-	3	7	-	7	-	-	17	5.92%
Scraper	1	4	10	13	-	6	2	4	40	13.93%
Notch	-	-	-	-	-	2	-	-	2	0.69%
Total	3 (1.04%)	11 (3.83%)	57 (19.86%)	114 (39.72%)	21 (7.31%)	68 (23.69&)	5 (1.74%)	8 (2.78%)	287	99.95%

In the above table, the site-wise and typology-wise analysis of microliths of Mesolithic period is presented. Total nine microlithic typology are found from eight sites, they are 69 fluted core, 41 flake, 99 blade, 3 awl, 9 borer, 7 burin, 17 points, 40 scraper and 2 notch. In respect to fluted core the Madhusudanpur locality-3 and College area contains highest numbers i.e. 23 and 21 respectively in comparison to other sites. Similarly the blade technology well developed in the Somakoi basin, the site College area and Balisahi represent 44 and 31 number of blade artefacts. The scraper is common typology in the collection but its representation very meager in comparison to other artefacts. The collection of burin, borer, points, notch, awl are limited in the somakoi basin.

NEOLITHIC:

Table 34: Type-wise distribution of Neoliths in Madhusudanpur locality-1

Name of the site	Typology	No	Percentage
Madhusudanpur locality-1	Axe	2	50%
	Blank	2	50%
Total		4	100%

According to this table four neoliths are found in Madhusudanpur locality-1 site. The details are included 2 blank and 2 axes.

Table 35: Type-wise distribution of Neoliths in Madhusudanpur locality-2

Name of the site	Typology	No	Percentage
Madhusudanpur locality-2	Axe	2	33.33%
	Blank	2	33.33%
	Flake	2	33.33%
Total		6	99.99%

In the above table 6 neoliths are found from Madhusudanpur locality-2 site for detail study purpose, which are included blank 2, axe 2 and flakes 2.

Table 36: Type-wise distribution of Neoliths in Madhusudanpur locality-3

Name of the site	Typology	No	Percentage
Madhusudanpur locality-3	Axe	4	10.81%
	Ring stone	7	18.91%
	Chisel	4	10.81%
	Hammer stone	2	5.40%
	Rubber stone	1	2.70%
	Flake	14	37.83%
	Blank	5	13.51%
Total		37	99.97%

Analysing the above table, there are seven types of neoliths are recovered from Madhusudanpur locality-3. The flake tool is found more in number. Besides the flake tool chisel 4, axe 4, ring stone 7, hammer stone 1 and rubber stone 1 are also found.

Table 37: Type-wise distribution of Neoliths in College Area

Name of the site	Typology	No	Percentage
College Area	Axe	3	8.33%
	Ring stone	17	47.22%
	Chisel	2	5.55%
	Hammer stone	5	13.88%
	Rubber stone	2	5.55%
	Flake	6	16.66%
	Blank	1	2.77%
Total		36	99.96%

In the above table indicate, 7 types of neoliths and total 36 tools are collected for study purpose. The implements included ring stone 17, hammer stone 5, rubber stone 2, chisel 2, axe 3, flake 6 and blank 1.

Table 38: Type-wise distribution of Neoliths in Tungur Pahar

Name of the site	Typology	No	Percentage
Tungur Pahar	Ring stone	3	16.66%
	Hammer stone	2	11.11%
	Quern	1	5.55%
	Polisher	1	5.55%
	Flake	8	44.44%
	Blank	3	16.66%
Total		18	99.97%

Above table shows the neolithic implements distribution of Tungur Pahar site. Total seven types and 18 neoliths are recovered from this site.

Table 39: Type-wise distribution of Neoliths in Balisahi

Name of the site	Typology	No	Percentage
Balisahi	Axe	4	21.05%
	Ring stone	3	15.78%
	Chisel	1	5.26%
	Cobble	2	10.52%
	Flake	9	47.36%
Total		19	99.97%

The above table shown there are five types of neoliths in Balisahi site collected for analytical study. Total 19 neoliths are recovered with dominant type of neolithic flake.

Table 40: Type-wise distribution of Neoliths in Kadalikund

Name of the site	Typology	No	Percentage
Kadalikund	Chisel	1	20%
	Polisher	1	20%
	Flake	1	20%
	Blank	2	40%
Total		5	100%

The above table indicates, there are four types of neoliths are found in Kadalikund site. Total five tools are collected.

Table 41: Type-wise distribution of Neoliths in Danduamunda

Name of the site	Typology	No	Percentage
Danduamunda	Flake	2	100%
Total		2	100%

In Danduamunda site two flakes are collected for study purpose.

Table 42: Type-wise distribution of Neoliths in Katarapali

Name of the site	Typology	No	Percentage
Katarapali	Ring stone	3	60%
	Rubber stone	1	20%
	Flake	1	20%
Total		5	100%

According to the above table three types of neoliths are found from Katarapali site. They are flake 1, ring stone 3 and rubber stone 1.

Table 43: Type-wise distribution of Neoliths in Nuagarh

Name of the site	Typology	No	Percentage
Nuagarh	Chisel	1	25%
	Ring stone	1	25%
	Polisher	2	50%
Total		4	100%

Above table shows the neolithic distribution in Nuagarh site. Total three types and four number of neoliths are recovered which includes chisel 1, ring stone 1 and polisher 2.

Table 44: Type-wise distribution of Neoliths in Telkoi

Name of the site	Typology	No	Percentage
Telkoi	Axe	1	1.17%
	Flake	42	49.41%
	Chips	42	49.41%
Total		85	99.99%

Analysing the above table, there are three types of neoliths are recovered from Telkoi site such as 1 axe, 42 flake and 42 chips. These large quantities of distribution of flakes and chips along with finish product on surface level attract author to systematic collection through grid method.

Table 45: Type-wise distribution of Neoliths in Gundurijhora

Name of the site	Typology	No	Percentage
Gundurijhora	Axe	1	100%
Total		1	100%

In Gundurijhora site only neolithic axe is found.

Table 46: Culture-wise and raw material-wise distribution of lithic materials

LOWER PALAEOLITHIC			UPPER PALAEOLITHIC			MESOLITHIC			NEOLITHIC		
Type	No	Percentage	Type	No	Percentage	Type	No	Percentage	Type	No	Percentage
Quartzite	24	100%	Quartzite	11	100%	Grey chert	69	24.04%	Dolorite	52	23.42%
						Quartz	25	8.71%	Diorite	117	52.70%
						Cherty Quartzite	43	14.98%	Sand stone	49	22.07%
						Black chert	107	37.28%	Shale	2	0.90%
						Banded Grey chert	3	1.04%	Quartz	2	0.90%
						Milky Quartz	13	4.52%			
						Iron ore	6	2.09%			
						Banded chert	7	2.43%			
						Crystal	3	1.04%			
						Banded cherty Quartz	1	0.34%			

						Banded Black chert	1	0.34%			
						Chert	2	0.69%			
						Vain chert	1	0.34%			
						Jasper	6 ?	2.09%			
Total	24	100%	Total	11	100%	Total	287	99.93%	Total	222	99.99%

The 24 lower Palaeolithic tools are from quartzite raw materials. Similarly the Upper Palaeolithic tools are made out of quartzite. The types of Mesolithic raw materials of 8 sites are milky quartz, chert, grey chert, cherty quartz, black chert, banded grey chert, Iron ore, banded black chert, vain chert and jasper (?).There are five types of raw material analysing basically Neolithic tool manufacturing. These are dolorite, diorite, sand stone, shale and quartz.

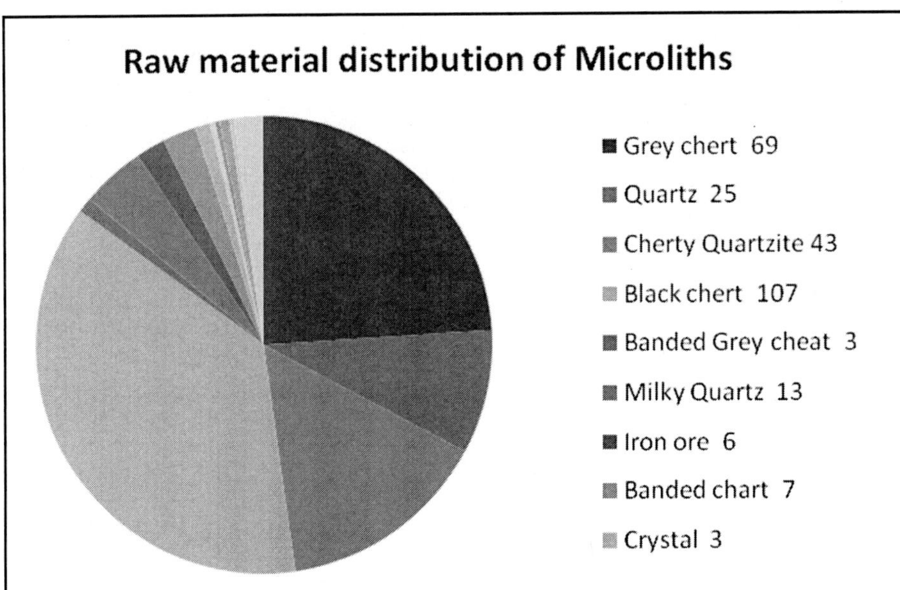

Fig-21: Pie chart representing raw material distribution of Microliths

Table 47: Site-wise and typology-wise analysis of artefacts (Neolithic)

Tool Type	Madhusudanpur locality-1	Madhusudanpur locality-2	Madhusudanpur locality-3	College Area	Tungurpahar	Balisahi	Kadalikund	Danduamunda	Katarapali	Nuagarh	Telkoi	Gundurijhora	No	Percentage
Axe	2	2	4	3	-	4	-	-	-	-	1	1	17	7.65%
Chisel	-	-	4	2	-	1	1	-	-	1	-	-	9	4.05%
Ring Stone	-	-	7	17	3	3	-	-	3	1	-	-	34	15.31%
Hammer Stone	-	-	2	5	2	-	-	-	-	-	-	-	9	4.05%
Quern	-	-	-	-	1	-	-	-	-	-	-	-	1	0.45%
Rubber Stone	-	-	1	2	-	-	-	-	1	-	-	-	4	1.80%
Cobble	-	-	-	-	-	2	-	-	-	-	-	-	2	0.90%
Polisher	-	-	-	-	1	-	1	-	-	2	-	-	4	1.80%
Blank	2	2	5	1	3	-	2	-	-	-	-	-	15	6.75%
Flake	-	2	14	6	8	9	1	2	1	-	42	-	85	38.28%
Chips	-	-	-	-	-	-	-	-	-	-	42	-	42	18.91%
Total	4 (1.80%)	6 (2.70%)	47 (21.17%)	36 (16.21%)	18 (8.10%)	19 (8.55%)	5 (2.25%)	2 (0.90%)	5 (2.25%)	4 (1.80%)	85 (38.28%)	1 (0.45%)	222	99.95%

In the above table, the site-wise and type-wise analysis of Neolithic is presented. Total eleven Neolithic typology are found from tweleve sites, they are 34 ring stone, 17 axe, 9 hammer stone, 4 rubber stone, 2 cobble, 4 polisher, 1 quern, 85 flake and 42 chips. In respect to ring stone the College area site contains highest numbers i.e 17 number in comparison to other sites. The Tungur Pahar site encounters a fragment of quern. The axe is well developed typology in the Somakoi basin. The Neolithic flake and chips are commonly available in almost all site in concentrate manner signify the tool manufacturing.

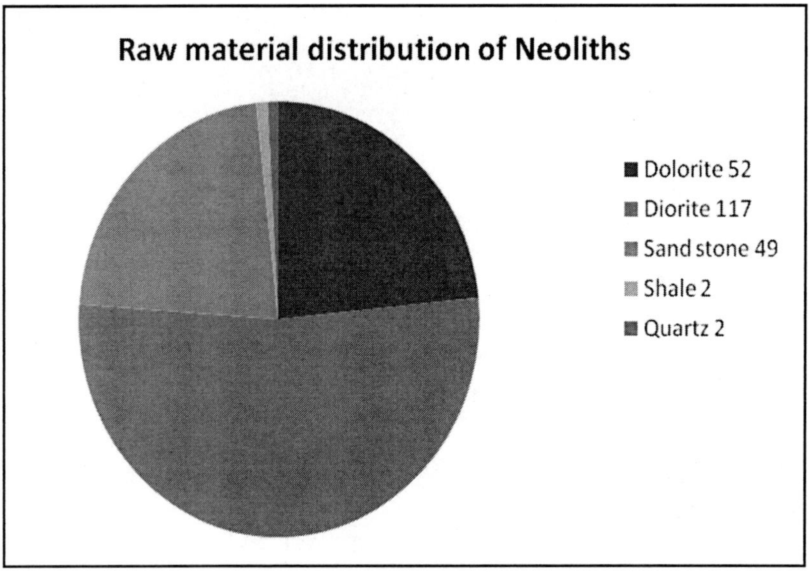

Fig-22: Pie chart representing raw material distribution of Neoliths

In the present Survey 12 sites are explored, out of which only one site i.e. Telkoi is surveyed by grid method. Because the site is least disturbed, and the decision was taken for trial trench. The grid laid out at the site is of 5x5m.The grid was divided into 25 units. Some are implementiferous and some are non-implementiferous. Both lithic and ceramic objects are recovered from the grid. Along with neolithic materials some microliths are also found. Therefore after the finding, the cultural period is divided into two segments i.e. Mesolithic and Neolithic.

CULTURE SEGMENTS (GRID)

(a) Mesolithic :

Mesolithic period in human cultural history is defined as the earliest Holocene culture that occurs before agriculture was started. Mesolithic period is the transitional phase between Palaeolithic and Neolithic. In this period pigmy tools were evolved named as microliths.

Since microliths show a basic principles of shedding mass drastically it is not illogical to believe that missiles might have resulted as a logical end of this technology. In the grid survey some microliths of Mesolithic period are found along with Neolithic materials.

(b) Neolithic :

As the youngest period of stone age history of man Neolithic has always been understood as a well defined stage. The concluding phase of the lithic culture is Neolithic period. Hence this period evidenced evolved typology and technology. The characteristic tools types from the grid materials are axe, flake and chips with some potsherds as associated materials.

These materials are analysed by the following table:-

Table 48: Distribution of materials at Telkoi grid

Grid unit	Recovery of lithic materials	No
A1	Chips	3
,,	Flake	1
A2	Chip	1
A3	Flake	1
,,	Chip	2
A5	Chip	3
B1	Chip	1
B2	Flake	4
,,	Chip	1
B3	Flake	1
B4	Flake	2
,,	Chip	1
B5	Chip	5
,,	Flake	1
C1	Flake	3
,,	Chip	1
C2	Flake	1
,,	Chip	7
C3	Flake	2

D1	Flake	5
D2	Flake	2
D3	Flake	1
D4	Flake	3
”	Chipped Bar Axe	1
”	Chip	1
D5	Flake	1
E1	Chip	2
E2	Chip	1
E3	Flake	1
”	Chip	2
Total		61

The above table shows the distribution of lithic materials of the grid at Telkoi.

Table 49: Distribution of Ceramics objects in the grid

Grid unit	Recovery of potsherds	Total No
A1	Body sherd	3
A2	Body sherd	2
A3	Body sherd	4
A4	Body sherd	1
A5	Body sherd	3
B1	Body sherd	2
B2	Body sherd	2
B3	Body sherd	3
B4	Body sherd	1
”	Brunt clay	1
C1	Body sherd	2
C2	Body sherd	6
C3	Rim sherd	1
”	Brunt clay	1
”	Body sherd	1
D1	Body sherd	1

D2	Body sherd	1
D4	Body sherd	1
E2	Body sherd	2
E3	Body sherd	2
E4	Rim sherd	1
E5	Body sherd	3
Total		44

The above table shows the distribution of ceramic objects in the Telkoi grid. The ceramic object include body sherd, rim sherd of pottery and few brunt clay are found.

From the 25 grid units of Telkoi site, only 19 units are evidenced ceramic and other objects i.e. potsherd and brunt clay and 42 potsherds are plotted and collected for the study purpose. The recovered potsherds are of red ware, undiagnostic, small in size and too fragmentary. So it is difficult to draw its details as drawing and description.

Table 47: Classification of Flakes and Chips of Telkoi Grid

Measurement of length (in cm)	No of flakes & chips
00-0.5	—
0.6-1.0	2
1.1-1.5	15
1.6-2.0	14
2.1-2.5	12
2.6-3.0	15
3.1-3.5	2
3.6-4.0	—
4.1-4.5	—
4.6-5.0	—
5.1-5.5	—
5.6-6.0	—
6.1-6.5	—
6.6-7.0	—
7.1-7.5	1
Total	61

According to the above table 61 flakes and chips are recovered from the grid. They are divided into 15 groups, out of which 8 groups do not have flakes and chips in this category. These groups are categorised on the basis of length measurement differences 0.5 cm. The materials measuring below 2 cm. are considered as chips and above 2 cm. are considered as different sizes of flakes. On the basis of size the big size flakes are less in number and small flakes are more in number.

METRIC ANALYSIS OF LITHIC TYPOLOGY

(a) Lower Palaeolithic

The lower Palaeolithic materials have been reported from Madhusudanpur locality-1, Madhusudanpur locality-3, College area, Tungur pahar, Nuagarh, Telkoi and Kadalikund site. The details of materials have been studied with reference to their rock type, typology, metric measurement and ratio.

The metric measurement such as length, breadth and thickness have been studied as per the standard measurement procedures. Attempt has been made to note the ratio of the measurement and they have been studied such as, B/L, T/L and T/B.

Table 51: Average metric data of distributed Lower Palaeolithic typology

Typology	No	Mean measurement in cm.			Mean ratio		
		L	B	T	B/L	T/L	T/B
Chopper	4	11.7	11.9	5.3	1.0	0.45	0.44
Hand axe	12	11.3	7.8	3.6	0.69	0.31	0.46
Cleaver	4	14.8	11.0	4.6	0.74	0.31	0.41
Flake	4	7.2	6.0	1.9	0.83	0.26	0.31

Analysing the table, it is observed that there are four lower palaeolithic typology consisting hand axe, chopper, cleaver and flakes. The average metric measurements of the typology and the ratio have been presented.

Table 52: Average metric measurement of Lower Palaeolithic in Madhusudanpur locality-1

Typology	No	Mean measurement in cm.			Mean ratio		
		L	B	T	B/L	T/L	T/B
Hand axe	3	8.7	7.1	4.1	0.81	0.47	0.57
Cleaver	1	10.1	10.6	3.5	1.04	0.34	0.33

In the above table observed that there are two types of lower palaeolithic tools consisting hand axe and cleaver. The average metric measurements of the typology and the ratio have been presented in the table.

Table 53: Average metric measurement of Lower Palaeolithic in College area

Typology	No	Mean measurement in cm.			Mean ratio		
		L	B	T	B/L	T/L	T/B
Hand axe	1	9.7	8.6	4.1	0.88	0.42	0.47
Chopper	1	8.2	10.1	5.1	1.23	0.62	0.50

In the above table observed that there are two types of lower palaeolithic tools consisting hand axe and chopper. The average metric measurements of the typology and the ratio have been presented in the table.

Table 54: Average metric measurement of Lower Palaeolithic typology Madhusudanpur locality-3.

Typology	No	Mean measurement in cm.			Mean ratio		
		L	B	T	B/L	T/L	T/B
Hand axe	1	16.8	10.3	4.5	0.61	0.26	0.43

Analysing the above table, one hand axe and its mean measurement and mean ratio is presented.

Table 55: Average metric measurement of Lower Palaeolithic typology in Tungur Pahar.

Typology	No	Mean measurement in cm.			Mean ratio		
		L	B	T	B/L	T/L	T/B
Chopper	1	10.8	10.2	4.9	0.94	0.45	0.48
Hand axe	1	13.3	8.9	3.9	0.66	0.29	0.43

In the above table, average metric mean measurement and mean ratio of two typologies have been presented.

Table 56: Average metric measurement of Lower Palaeolithic typology in Kadalikund.

Typology	No	Mean measurement in cm.			Mean ratio		
		L	B	T	B/L	T/L	T/B
Chopper	2	13.9	13.8	5.7	0.99	0.41	0.41
Hand axe	6	12.5	7.4	3.5	0.59	0.28	0.47
Cleaver	3	17.1	11.3	5.2	0.67	0.31	0.46

Analysing the above table, it is observed that there are three lower palaeolithic typology consisting hand axe, chopper, and cleaver. The average metric measurements of the typology and the ratio have been presented in the table.

Table 57: Average metric measurement of Lower Palaeolithic typology in Nuagarh.

Typology	No	Mean measurement in cm.			Mean ratio		
		L	B	T	B/L	T/L	T/B
Flake	2	8.5	6.3	2.1	0.74	0.24	0.33

Analysing the above table, there average metric measurement and mean ratio is presented.

Table 58: Average metric measurement of Lower Palaeolithic typology in Telkoi

Typology	No	Mean measurement in cm.			Mean ratio		
		L	B	T	B/L	T/L	T/B
Flake	2	5.8	5.8	1.8	1.0	0.31	0.31

In the above table, there are two flakes. The average metric measurements of the typology and the ratio have been presented in the table.

(b) Upper Palaeolithic

The upper Palaeolithic materials have been reported from Madhusudanpur locality-3. The details of materials have been studied with reference to their rock type, typology, metric measurement and ratio.

The metric measurements such as length, breadth and thickness have been studied as per the standard measurement procedures. Attempt has been made to note the ratio of the measurement and they have been studied such as, B/L, T/L and T/B.

Table 59: Average metric measurement of Upper Palaeolithic typology in Madhusudanpur locality-3

Typology	No	Mean measurement in cm.			Mean ratio		
		L	B	T	B/L	T/L	T/B
Scraper	4	8.4	6.6	2.7	0.78	0.32	0.40
Flake	4	4.7	3.3	1.0	0.70	0.21	0.30
Blade	2	7.3	4.0	1.3	0.54	0.17	0.32
Nodule	1	8.7	4.8	3.3	0.55	0.37	0.68

In the above table the upper palaeolithic typologies are presented in an evolutionary order, Total four typology are found, these are flake, scraper, blade and nodule.The average metric measurements and mean ratio of the typology have been presented.

(c) Mesolithic

The mesolithic materials have been reported from Madhusudanpur locality-1, Madhusudanpur locality-2, Madhusudanpur locality-3, College area, Tungur Pahar, Balisahi, Nuagarh and Telkoi, The details of materials have been studied with reference to their rock type, typology, metric measurement and ratio.

The metric measurements such as length, breadth and thickness have been studied as per the standard measurement procedures. Attempt has been made to note the ratio of the measurement and they have been studied as B/L, T/L and T/B.

Table 60: Average metric data distributed Mesolithic typology.

Typology	No	Mean measurement in cm.			Mean ratio		
		L	B	T	B/L	T/L	T/B
Scraper	40	3.4	6.6	2.7	0.78	0.32	0.40
Fluted core	69	3.2	2.1	1.6	0.65	0.5	076
Flake	41	3.8	2.7	0.8	0.71	0 21	0 29
Borer	9	3.6	1.1	0.6	0.30	0.16	014
Burin	7	3.5	2.3	0.8	0.66	0.22	0 31
Awl	3	2.4	1.5	0.8	0.62	0.33	0.53
Point	17	3.1	1.4	0.5	0.45	0.16	0 35
Notch	2	2.3	2.1	0.7	0.91	0.30	0.33
Backed blade	9	2.5	0.9	0.3	0.36	0.12	0.33
Parallel sided blade	33	2.8	1.1	0.4	0.39	0.14	0.36
Single sided blade	7	3.1	2.4	0.4	0.77	0.12	0.16
Denticulated blade	1	2.1	1.0	0.4	0.47	0.19	0.4
Double sided blade	16	4.5	1.2	0.3	0.26	0.06	0.25
Blade	33	3.6	1.8	0.7	0.5	0.19	0.38

In the above table the microliths typology are presented in an evolutionary order. Total 14 typologies are found. They are scraper, fluted core, flake, borer, burin, awl, point, notch, backed blade, parallel sided blade, single sided blade, denticulated blade, double sided blade and simple blade. The average metric measurement and mean ratio of the typologies have been presented.

Table 61: Average metric measurement of microliths typology in Madhusudanpur locality-1

Typology	No	Mean measurement in cm.			Mean ratio		
		L	B	T	B/L	T/L	T/B
Fluted core	2	3.6	1.8	1.2	0.5	0.33	1.5
Scraper	1	4.3	3.7	3.1	0.86	0.72	0.83

Analysing the above table, it is observed that there are two numbers of microliths typology in Madhusudanpur locality-1 site. The average metric measurements and mean ratio of the typology have been shown in the table.

Table 62: Average metric measurement of microliths typology in Madhusudanpur locality-2

Typology	No	Mean measurement in cm			Mean ratio		
		L	B	T	B/L	T/L	T/B
Fluted core	1	2.2	1.6	1.1	0.72	0.50	0.68
Flake	4	4.4	2.6	0.9	0.59	0.20	0.34
Scraper	4	3.0	2.8	0.8	0.93	0.26	0.28
Backed blade	1	2.4	1.7	0.6	0.70	0.25	0.35
Blade	1	2.2	1.0	0.4	0.45	0.18	0.4

The above table, the average metric measurements, ratio of the mesolithic of Madhusudanpur locality-2 site with their systematic arrangement have been presented.

Table 63: Average metric measurement of microliths typology in Madhusudanpur locality-3

Typolog y	No	Mean measurement in cm			Mean ratio		
		L	B	T	B/L	T/L	T/B
Fluted core	23	3.1	2.2	1.4	0.70	0.45	0.63
Flake	3	3.8	2.1	1.0	0.55	0.26	0.47
Scraper	10	3.1	2.7	1.2	0.87	0.38	0.44
Blade	15	2.6	1.1	0.4	0.42	0.15	0.36
Point	3	3.2	1.8	0.6	0.56	0.18	0.33
Awl	1	2.9	1.2	0.8	0.41	0.27	0.66
Borer	2	3.4	1,2	0.5	0.35	0.14	0.41

Analysing the table, it is observed that there are 7 typology of Mesolithic period in Mashusudanpur locality-3. The above table has shown the average metric measurements and the ratio of typology.

Table 64: Average metric measurement of microliths typology in College area

Typology	No	Mean measurement in cm.			Mean ratio		
		L	B	T	B/L	T/L	T/B
Fluted core	21	3.6	2.2	1.7	0.61	0.47	0.77
Flake	17	3.4	3.2	0.9	0.84	0.23	0.28
Scraper	13	3.4	3.2	1.7	0.94	0.5	0.53
Blade	44	3.2	1.2	0.5	0.37	0.15	0.41

Point	7	2.8	1.1	0.4	0.39	0.14	0.36
Awl	2	2.7	1.2	0.7	0.44	0.25	0.58
Borer	3	4.4	1.1	0.7	0.25	0.15	0.65
Burin	7	3.5	2.3	0.8	0.65	0.22	0.34

According to the above table there are 8 typology of mesolithic culture in College area site. The metric measurements and ratio have been given and the typology are presented with their evolutionary order.

Table 65: Average metric measurement of microliths typology in Tungur Pahar.

Typology	No	Mean measurement in cm.			Mean ratio		
		L	B	T	B/L	T/L	T/B
Fluted core	10	3.1	2.2	1.3	0.70	0.41	0.59
Flake	5	4.2	2.6	0.9	0.61	0.21	0.34
Blade	5	4.6	1.8	0.7	0.39	0.15	0.38
Borer	1	2.7	1.0	0.4	0.37	0.14	0.4

The above table shows the distribution of mesolithic culture tool typology and their average and metric measurements and mean ratio.

Table 66: Average metric measurement of microlithic typology in Balisahi.

Typology	No	Mean measurement in cm.			Mean ratio		
		L	B	T	B/L	T/L	T/B
Fluted core	9	3.5	2.2	1.6	0.62	0.45	0.72
Flake	10	3.4	2.0	0.6	0.58	0.17	0.3
Blade	31	2.7	1.1	0.4	0.40	0.14	0.36
Scraper	6	4.1	2.8	1.6	0.68	0.39	0.57
Borer	3	3.2	1.0	0.7	0.31	0.21	0.7
Point	7	3.4	1.6	0.7	0.47	0.20	0.43
Notch	2	2.7	1.6	0.7	0.59	0.25	0.43

In the above table the average metric measurement and ratio of the microliths typology have been presented. Seven microliths typology are found from this site.

Table 67: Average metric measurement of microliths typology in Nuagarh

Typology	No	Mean measurement in cm			Mean ratio		
		L	B	T	B/L	T/L	T/B
Fluted core	1	6.3	1.7	1.6	0.26	0.25	0.94
Flake	1	2.7	1.9	0.6	0.70	0.22	0.31
Blade	1	3.0	1.4	0.5	0.46	0.16	0.35
Scraper	2	3.8	3.1	1.1	0.81	0.28	0.35

The above table shows the distribution of microliths typology and their average and metric measurements and ratio of the Nuagarh site.

Table 68: Average metric measurement of microliths typology in Telkoi

Typology	No	Mean measurement in cm.			Mean ratio		
		L	B	T	B/L	T/L	T/B
Fluted core	2	3.2	3.3	2.0	1.03	0.62	0.60
Flake	1	3.7	2.3	0.9	0.62	0.24	0.39
Blade	1	2.9	1.7	0.9	0.58	0.31	0.52
Scraper	4	3.4	2.7	1.3	0.79	0.38	0.48

The above table shows the distribution of microliths typology of mesolithic period of the Telkoi site. Further their average metric measurements and ratio have also been presented.

(d) Neolithic

The Neolithic materials have been, reported from different sites around Telkoi. The details of Neolithic materials have been studied with reference to their rock type, typology, metric measurement and ratio.

The metric measurements such as length, breadth and thickness have been studied as per the standard measurement procedures. The length has been considered from the stand to working end, breadth of maximum breadth and thickness at maximum thickness levels. The measurements have been represented by length as L, breadth as B and thickness as T. The ratio been studied such as B/L, T/L and T/B.

The distribution of Neolithic and their metric measurements have been studied in general and for individual sites and they are presented as follows:

Table 69: Average metric measurement of Neolithic typology in Madhusudanpur locality-1

Typology	No	Mean measurement in cm			Mean ratio		
		L	B	T	B/L	T/L	T/B
Axe	2	8.0	4.4	1.1	0.55	0.13	0.25
Blank	2	11.1	6.3	4.1	0.56	0.36	0.65

Here in this table the neolithic typology include axe and blank. There average metric measurement and mean ratio have been presented.

Table 70: Average metric measurement of Neolithic typology in Madhusudanpur locality-2

Typology	No	Mean measurement in cm			Mean ratio		
		L	B	T	B/L	T/L	T/B
Axe	2	6.4	3.4	1.3	0.53	0.20	0.38
Flake	2	7.5	5.4	1.9	0.72	0.25	0.35
Blank	2	9.0	7.6	4.3	0.84	0.47	0.56

In the table, the typology of neolithic period represents are axe, blank and flake. The average metric measurements and mean ratio of the typology have been presented.

Table 71: Average metric measurement of Neolithic typology in Madhusudanpur locality-3

Typology	No	Mean measurement in cm			Mean ratio		
		L	B	T	B/L	T/L	T/B
Axe	4	10.6	4.8	2.6	0.45	0.24	0.54
Flake	14	6.6	3.9	1.1	0.59	0.16	0.28
Chisel	4	7.0	2.9	2.1	0.41	0.3	0.72
Ring Stone	7	11.7	5.9	5.8	0.50	0.49	0.98
Hammer stone	2	7.7	5.7	4.6	0.74	0.59	0.80
Rubber stone	1	8.1	7.5	2.8	0.92	0.34	0.37
Blank	5	10.3	7.1	5.2	0.68	0.53	0.73

Above table represent the neolithic typology of Madhusudanpur locality-3. The site is presented axe, chisel, flake, blank, ring stone, hammer stone and rubber stone. The average metric measurements and mean ratio of the typology have been shown.

Table 72: Average metric measurement of Neolithic typology in College Area

Typology	No	Mean measurement in cm			Mean ratio		
		L	B	T	B/L	T/L	T/B
Axe	3	12.9	5.4	2.6	0.41	0.20	0.48
Flake	6	4.6	2.8	0.8	0.60	0.17	0.28
Chisel	2	5.7	2.8	1.8	0.49	0.31	0.64
Ring Stone	17	10.1	6.3	5.3	0.62	0.52	0.84
Hammer stone	5	9.1	6.7	5.8	0.73	0.63	0.86
Rubber stone	2	11.2	9.5	6.2	0.84	0.55	0.65
Blank	1	9.3	5.5	4.8	0.59	0.51	0.87

Analysing the above table, it is observed that seven types of neolithic typology reported in College area site. The average metric measurements and mean ratio of the typology have been presented.

Table 73: Average metric measurement of Neolithic typology in Tungur Pahar

Typology	No	Mean measurement in cm			Mean ratio		
		L	B	T	B/L	T/L	T/B
Flake	7	7.8	5.0	1.9	0.64	0.24	0.38
Ring Stone	3	8.9	4.1	4.5	0.46	0.50	1.09
Hammer stone	2	7.1	5.6	4.2	0.78	0.59	0.75
Quern	2	20.6	15.6	5.8	0.75	0.28	0.37
Polisher	1	8.7	7.2	4.6	0.82	0.52	0.63
Blank	3	10.5	6.9	4.3	0.65	0.40	0.62

In the above table six neolithic typology are presented. They are blank, flake, ring stone, hammer stone, quern and polisher. The average metric measurement and mean ratio of the typology has been presented.

Table 74: Average metric measurement of Neolithic typology in Balisahi

Typology	No	Mean measurement in cm			Mean ratio		
		L	B	T	B/L	T/L	T/B
Axe	4	15.4	4.5	2.4	0.29	0.15	0.53
Chisel	1	6.7	2.8	2.0	0.41	0.29	0.71
Flake	9	3.5	3.1	0.8	0.88	0.22.	0.25
Ring stone	3	8.4	5.7	3.9	0.67	0.46	0.68
Cobble	2	12.9	8.5	7.5	0.65	0.58	0.88

According to the above table there are five typology of neolithic in Balisahi site. The metric measurements and ratio have been given and the typology are presented.

Table 75: Average metric measurement of Neolithic typology in Kadalikund

Typology	No	Mean measurement in cm			Mean ratio		
		L	B	T	B/L	T/L	T/B
Flake	1	7.5	3.5	0.8	0.46	0.10	0.22
Chisel	1	7.0	3.9	2.6	0.55	0.37	0.66
Polisher	1	10.2	6.9	3.9	0.67	0.38	0.56
Blank	2	14.2	8.1	6.5	0.57	0.45	0.81

The above table shows the distribution of neolithic typology and their average metric measurements and mean ratio of the Kadalikund site.

Table 76: Average metric measurement of Neolithic typology in Danduamunda

Typology	No	Mean measurement in cm			Mean ratio		
		L	B	T	B/L	T/L	T/B
Flake	2	3.8	3.0	0.7	0.78	0.18	0.23
Ring stone	1	10.2	5.8	5.0	0.56	0.49	0.86

Analysing the above table, the average metric measurement and mean ratio of the neolithic typology have been presented. Two neolithic typology are found from this site.

Table 77: Average metric measurement of Neolithic typology in Katarapali

Typology	No	Mean measurement in cm			Mean ratio		
		L	B	T	B/L	T/L	T/B
Flake	1	5.6	4.1	1.6	0.73	0.28	0.39
Ring stone	3	8.7	4.8	4.5	0.55	0.51	0.93
Rubber stone	1	7.2	7.2	5.0	1.0	0.69	0.69

In the table, the neolithic typology of Katarapali site are presented. They are flake, ring stone and rubber stone.

Table 78: Average metric measurement of Neolithic typology in Nuagarh

Typology	No	Mean measurement in cm			Mean ratio		
		L	B	T	B/L	T/L	T/B
Chisel	1	7.3	3.5	2.5	0.68	0.34	0.71
Ring stone	1	11.3	6.8	6.2	0.60	0.54	0.91
Polisher	2	11.9	8.6	5.3	0.72	0.44	0.17

The above table represent three categories of neolithic typology in Nuagarh site. The metric measurement and mean ratio have been given and the typology are presented with their evolutionary order.

Table 79: Average metric measurement of Neolithic typology in Telkoi

Typology	No	Mean measurement in cm			Mean ratio		
		L	B	T	B/L	T/L	T/B
Axe	1	7.4	4.2	2.3	0.56	0.31	0.54
Flake	42	3.9	3.1	0.9	0.79	0.23	0.29
Chips	42	1.9	1.5	0.4	0.78	0.21	0.26

The above table shows the distribution of neolithic typology, average metric measurements and mean ratio of the Telkoi site findings.

DESCRIPITON OF SELECTED ARTEFACTS

Lower Palaeolithic: It is the earliest cultural phase in the evolutionary sequence of prehistoric culture. The people of this phase were mainly hunter-gathers. The characteristic tools of this period were hand axe, cleaver, chopper etc. This cultural stage in India can neither be conceived of as chronologically homogeneous nor can one think of the cultural phase as uniformly occurring all over the country. In different parts of the subcontinent different zones/trends of this culture occur at different times. From the present survey hand axe, cleaver and chopper are found.

Upper Palaeolithic : Upper Palaeolithic culture has a distinct and wide spread distribution in several parts of the old world. By the definition the Upper Palaeolithic comprises lithic blade tools and bone tool technology chronologically it is a culture of Terminal Pleistocene and authors were homo-sapience sapience. They represent a marked and fairly consistent change in method of making stone tool and their use. In present survey a few number of upper palaeolithic artefacts have been found such as blade, flake and scraper. The blades in general have one or two mid ridge on the drosal surfaces indeterminate flakes. They are long and inform and sometimes irregular the working end.

Mesolithic : The man of this period produced compound tools called microliths. Mesolithic period is a transitional stage between palaeolithic and neolithic which were lifted into convenient handle and used for various purposes. Microliths are of various type determined according to the deliberately given to them by man while fashioning them further by trimming the edges by retouch. The different tools types are cores, blades, micro burin, borers, lunate and scraper etc.

Neolithic : In the cultural history of mankind the Neolithic age marks the concluding phase of the stone tool culture. Neolithic age is characterised by the introduction of more evolved and developed typological features. A characteristic feature of this age is evaluation of grounding and polishing of stones. The tool is usually smooth and robbed at edges. The tool typology which are included in this age are celt, axe, adze, ring stones, chisels, flakes, grinding and rubbing stones. The rocks on which the technique of grounding has been extensively employed by man were all fine grained rocks such as basalt, dolorite etc.

Description of drawing artefacts :

CA-154, Axe; 10.7 x 4.1x 2.3 cm and weight is 283 gm. The tool is triangular and round cutting edge and raw material is dolorite.

MP-1 03, Chisel; 6.1 x 2.1 x 1.6 cm and weight is 45gm. The tool is made out of fine grain granite and shape is rectangular.

TP-36, Ring stone; 13.3 x6.1 x 5.5 cm and weight is 865 gm. The shape is oval and the raw material is sand stone.

TP-41, Polisher; 8.7 x 7.2 x 4.6 cm and weight is 495 gm. The shape is oval and the raw material is sand stone.

BS-81, Chipped bar axe; 18.8 x 5.4x 2.7 cm and weight is 318 gm. The shape of the chipped bar axe is trapezoid and raw material is dolorite.

BS-84, Axe; 10.0x 4.1 x 2.1 cm and weight is 108gm. The working end is straight and raw material of the tool is dolorite.

KK-2, Chopper; 11.1 x 9.8 x 4.9 cm and weight is 632 gm. The shape of the tool is roundish and raw material is quartzite.

KK-3-Hand axe; 14.3 x 9.5 x 4.7 cm and weight is 684 gm. The shape of the tool is acuminate flakes are notice from periphery to centre. Raw material of the tool is quartzite.

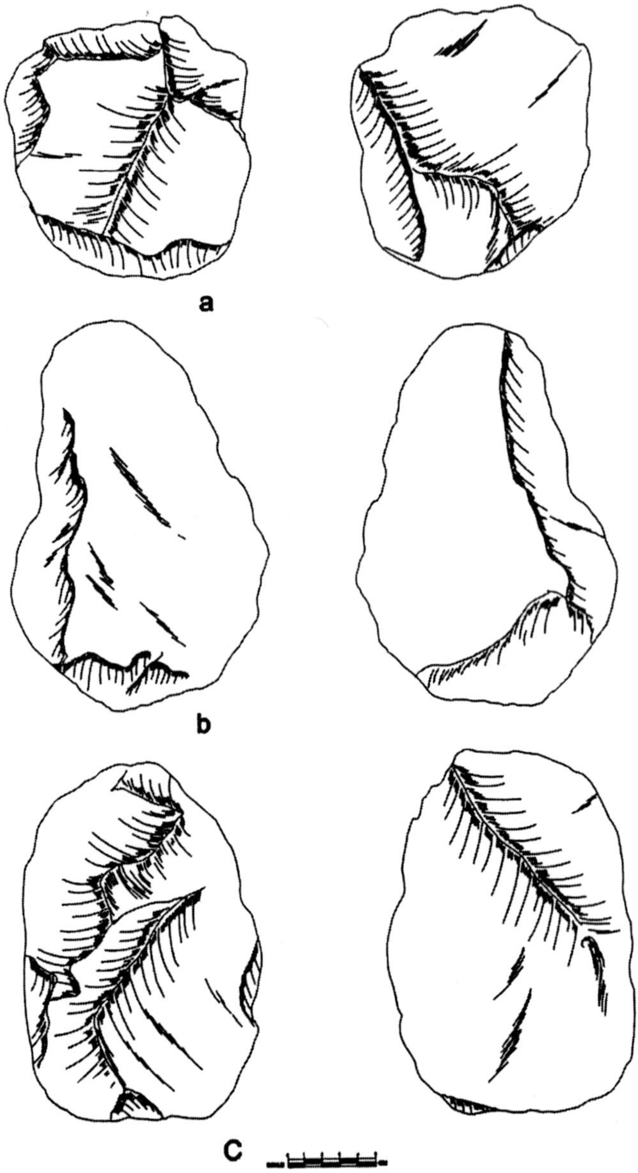

(a)KK-2; Copper, (b)KK-3; Hand Axe and (c)KK-3; Hand Axe

Fig-23: Palaeolithic artefacts from Kadalikund.

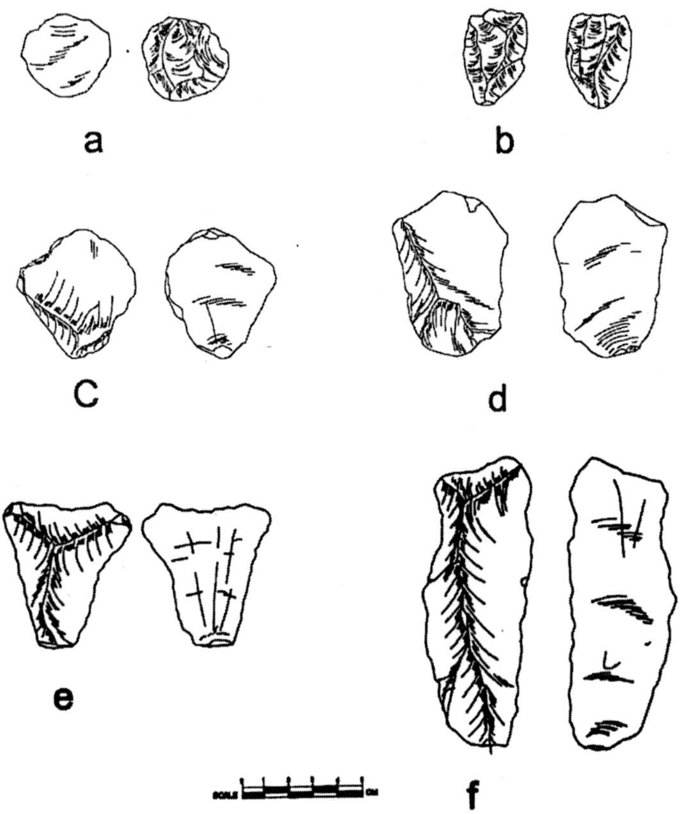

(a)TK-8; Notch (b)NG-4; Blade (c)NG-6; End Scraper (d)TK-14; Neolithic Flake (e)TK-29; Neolithic Flake (f)TK-29; Neolithic Flake

Fig-24: Microlithic and Neolithic artefacts from Nuagarh and Telkoi.

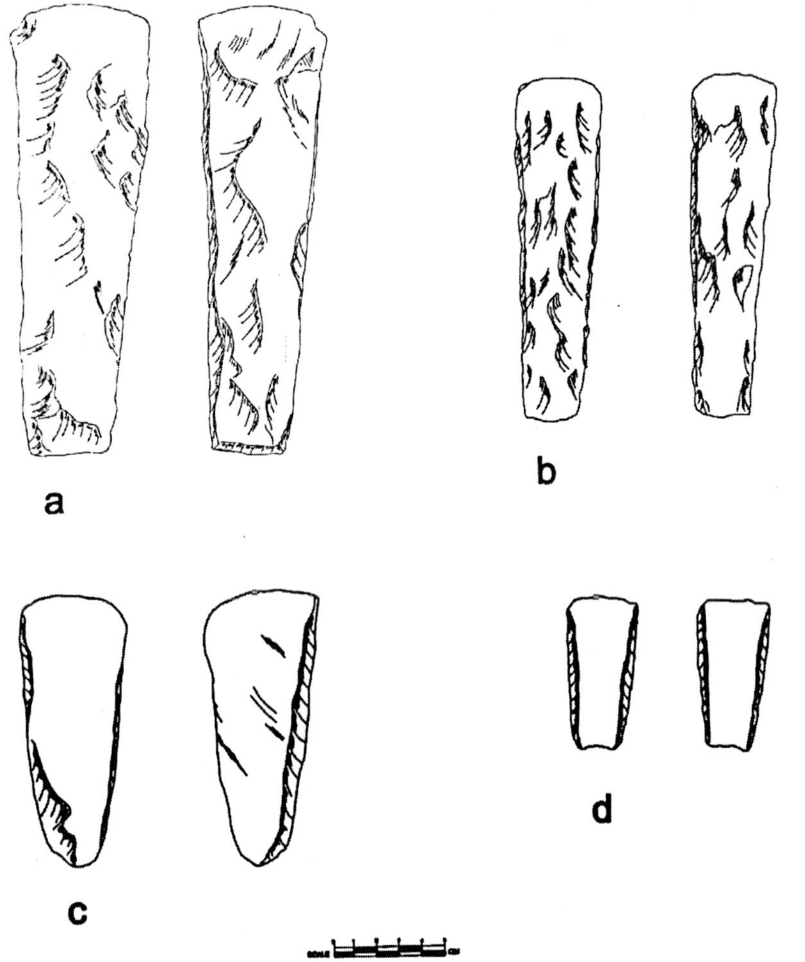

(a)BS-81; Chipped Bar Axe, (b)BS-84; Axe,(c)CA-154; Axe (d)MP-103;Chisel

Fig-25: Neolithic artefacts from Balisahi, College area and Madhusudanpur locality-1.

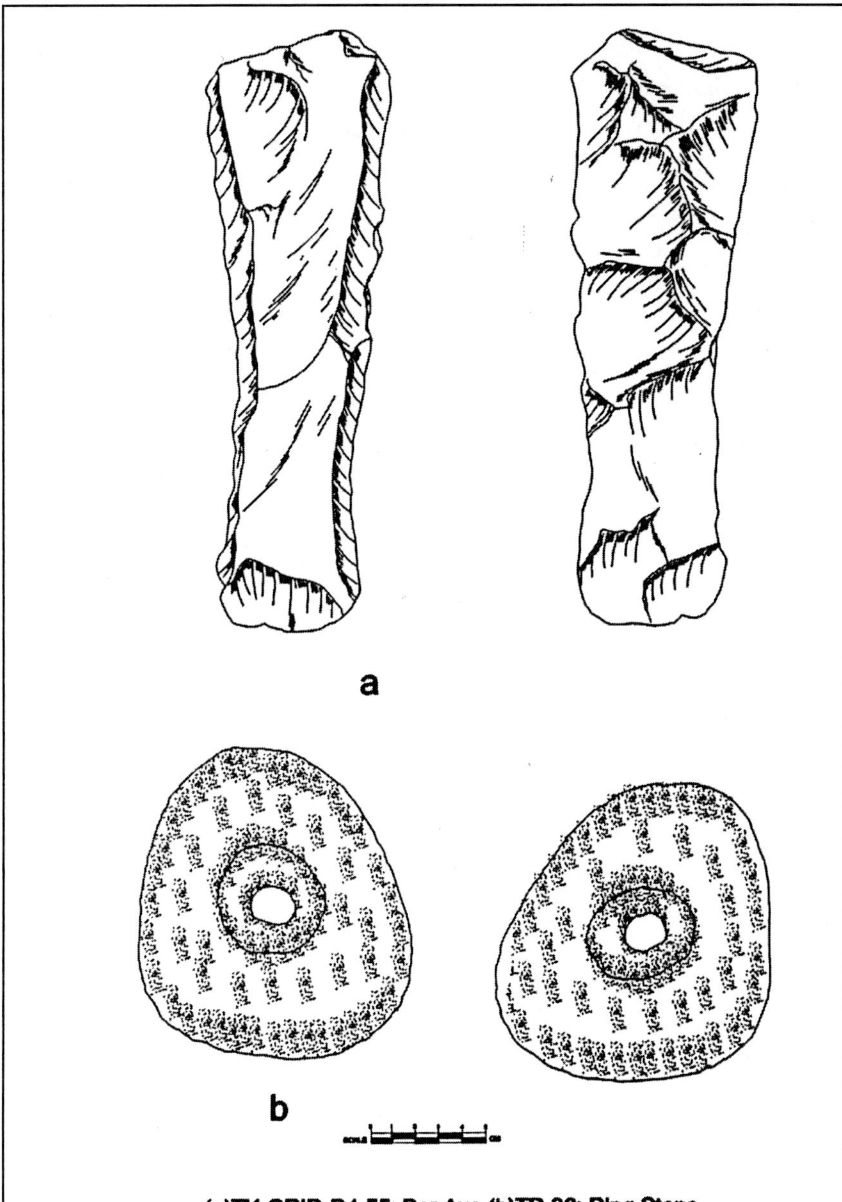

Fig-26: Neolithic artefacts from Telkoi and Tungur pahar.

KK-4, Hand axe; 11.5 x 7.6 x 3.0 cm and weight is 323 gm. The tool is made out of quartzite. The shape of the tool is limande. A longitudinal side are zigzag and sharp.

NG-4, Blade; 3.0 x 1.4 x 0.5 cm and weight is 15gm. The shape is elongated and raw material is grey chert.

NG-6, End scraper; 3.2 x 2.2 x 1.0 cm and weight is 9 gm. The shape of the tool is quadrilateral. Raw material of the tool is cherty quartzite.

TK-8, Notch; 2.5 x 2.1 x 0.9 cm and weight is 37 gm. It is Irregular in shape.

TK-11, Flake; 7.9 x 3.6 x 1.0 cm and weight is 35gm. It is elongated in shape and raw material is dolorite.

TK-14, Flake; 5.8 x 4.1 x 0.9 cm and weight is 21 gm. Shape of the flake is oval.

TK-29, Flake; 5.1 x 4.6 x 10 cm and weight is 16 gm. It is triangular in shape.

TK-GRID D4-55, Bar axe; 20.8 x 8.0 x 3.3 cm and weight is 390 gm. The shape of the bar axe is elongated and raw material is dolorite.

Main features of material cultures of Somakoi Basin

This chapter contains an account of Lower palaeolithic, Upper Palaeolithic, Mesolithic and Neolithic recoveries from my survey in the Somakoi Basin of Telkoi region. With regards to the upper Palaeolithic culture, only one site (Madhusudanpur Locality-3) has been reported eleven artefacts. On the other hand eight sites encounter with microlithic artefacts, seven site reported Lower Palaeolithic artefacts and twelve site noticed neolithic artefacts. This implies that during neolithic period, the Somakoi Basin become an important destination of prehistoric man. Hence, it is relevant to discuss the major characteristics of Palaeolithic, Mesolithic and Neolithic culture of Somakoi Basin which are as follow:

1. The Surveyed area has reported 24 (4.41%) specimen of lower Palaeolithic followed by 11 (2.02%) Upper Palaeolithic period, 287 (52.75%) Mesolithic period and 222 (40.80%) artefacts

of Neolithic period inferred the continuous occupation of the river basin by the prehistoric people.

2. The Lower Palaeolithic artefacts have been classified into four categories as per it typo-technological features such are as hand axe (12; 50%), chopper (4; 16.66%), cleaver (4; 16.66%) and flake (4; 16.66%).
3. The Upper Palaeolithic artefacts are very limited and only one site represent scraper, flake, nodule and blade implements.
4. The microlithic artefacts have been divided into nine typology which includes fluted core (69; 24.04%), flake (41; 14.28%), blade (99; 34.49%), awl (3; 1.04%), borer (9; 3.13%), burin (7; 2.43%), point (17; 5.92%), scraper (40; 13.93%) and notch (2; 0.69%). An important feature is that the Somakoi basin culture has a well-developed blade technology.
5. On the basis of general characteristics of morphological and typo-technological features, the neolithic collection are typologically classified as axe (17; 7.65%), chisel (9; 4.05%), ring stone (34; 15.31%), hammer stone (9; 4.05%), quern (1; 0.45%), rubber stone (4; 1.80%), polisher (4; 1.80%), blank (15; 6.75%), flake (85; 38.28%) and chips (42; 18.91%). The intensive survey in both side of the river and in around Telkoi block area resulted the discovery of 12 neolithic sites.
6. In order to study neolithic typology the axe and chisel are important in celt component, ring stone and hammer stone are large assemblage fall under pebble component. Another important feature is all the neolithic assemblages are made out of dolerite and diorite.

In the next chapter, archaeological recoveries through trial trench and historical period will be discussed.

CHAPTER 4

THE SITE AND EXCAVATION

The excavated site at Telkoi is situated near Dandasanali and river Somakoi confluence on right side of the road which runs from Telkoi to Kaliahota, in North-South direction, is 2 km in southern from Telkoi town. It is an eroded Jungle area and close to this river Somakoi.

The site has been selected for excavation of a trial trench because it is a flat and least disturbed surface and the clear evidence of neolithic chips, flakes, potsherds and one unfinished bar celt found in grid area. Also some neolithic belong to the intermediate manufacturing stage are also found in the erosional site near the grid. These have some chipping activities. It may be stated that this site may be a primary and factory one. So, it was decided for trial trench excavation, to know about the stratification and nature of deposition of artefacts.

During the period of trial excavation, the author followed the vertical excavation method. Two trial trenches were excavated at Telkoi site. These trenches were named R1 and R2. The trench R1 is 2 x 2m and R2 is 1 x 1 m. Before excavating these trenches, site is plotted the datum point (locate the cement pillar), which is maintained the boundary of Telkoi block forest division. This is situated near the confluence of Somakoi and Dandasanali rivers. The trench R1 is situated 27.92 m. distance in north-western direction from the datum point, further the trench R2 is 62.7 m distance western direction from R1 trench.

RECOVERY MATERIALS, LITHICS AND CERAMICS

Trench -RI

The site at Telkoi was studied by laying out a grid measuring 5 x 5 m. and plotted the distribution of cultural relics, from where the distribution of different artefacts were found primary in nature. The concentration of artefacts, which cover comprising 2 x 2 m area (2 x 2 m grid unit) was selected for excavation. From the datum point, the trench R1 was 27.92 m in North West and trench R2 was 62.7m in western direction respectively.

From the nature of distribution it may be suggested that the area was primarily associated with a distribution of neolithic relic of primary or secondary in nature. In order to examine the nature of surface distribution an excavation was under taken at Telkoi. It was proposed to observe the distribution of palaeo-relics and other distribution, briefly in depth-wise.

The following descriptions is given serially on the basis of depth-wise from Surface.

1. **Surface** - The total grid was scanned for the surface distribution details and it was observed that there was prehistoric relics at the area, one of which least distributed. This one is selected for trial trench, consist of grid unit D4, D5, E4 & E5. From this grid units one axe, few flakes and chips have been collected.
2. **Surface - 0.15 m :** During the excavation, the 0.15 m. depth from surface was critically examined in order to observe any change of soil deposition or the possible recovery of palaeo-relics. There were 1 flake, 2 chips and some potsherd reported. The recovered potsherds are too fragmentary. The flake which measure 2.8 x 1.6 x 0.6 cm, was made of dolerite.

3. **0.15 - 0.20 m :** The next step of excavation continued depth between 0.15 to 0.20m. 3 chips and 32 potsherds mainly comprise of 29 bodysherds and 3 rims sherd recovered from third depth. The potsherds are too fragmentary.
4. **0.20 - 0.25 m :** The depth between 0.20 to 0.25 m 3 flakes, 5 chips and 32 potsherd have been recovered. The flakes measure respectively 2.9 x 2.2 x 0.6 cm with 3.0gm, 2.6 x 3.2 x 0.5 cm with 3.5 gm. 2.5 x 2.5 x 0.6 cm with 3.2 gm made out of dolerite. All potsherds are too fragmentary of body part and of red ware.
5. **0.25 - 0.30 m :** The depth between 0.25 to 0.30 has yielded 18 flakes, 15 chips and 12 potsherds. The soil colour is slightly changed than the previous layer. The flakes are as possible more as the previous finding. The rock type of the flakes and chips are dolerite. The potsherds are too fragmentary and bodysherds of red ware.
6. **0.30 - 0.35 m :** From the excavation between 0.30m to 0.35m. depth 15 flakes, 9 chips and 2 potsherds have been recovered. The neolithic flakes are quite similar type as the previous finding. The rock types of the flakes are dolerite. The recovered potsherds are too fragmentary in nature and without any rim parts.
7. **0.35 - 0.40 m :** Excavation was made upto the 0.40m depth and it was critically examined in order to observe any change in soil deposition of the possible recovery of palaeo-relics. From this depth 6 flakes, 12 chips and 1 body sherd have been recovered. Rock type of the neolithic flake and chips is dolerite.
8. **0.40 - 0.45 m :** Further excavation between 0.40 to 0.45m depth, 3 number of neolithic flakes have been recorded. The flakes measures respectively 3.0 x 1.8 x 0.6 cm with 2.5gm, 2.4 x 2.9 x 0.4 cm with 3.5gm and 2.5 x 1.6 x 0.4 cm with 2.5gm. No ceramic remains have been reported from this depth.
9. **0.45 - 0.50 m :** Next lot of excavation conducted between 0.45 to 0.50m depth and it was critically examined in order to observe any change in soil nature, composition of the possible recovery of palaeo-relics. From this depth 2 neolithic chips of dolerite have been reported.

10. **0.50 - 0.55 m :** The depth between 0.50 to 0.55 m. yielded 1 neolithic flake which measured 2.3 x 2.1 x 0.7 cm with 3.8 gm. Rock type of the flake is dolerite. Soil sample was also collected from this lot for the purpose of pedological analysis.
11. **0.55-0.60 m:** Further excavation between 0.55 to 0.60 m was critically examined. No palaeo-relics has been reported from this depth. Soil sample was collected from this lot for the purpose of pedological analysis.

Table 80: Lot wise distribution of material from Trial Trench (R1)

Layer	Lot No	Depth (from surface in m.)	Level (from datum point in m.)	Lithic Material		Ceramics
				Flake	Chips	Potsherds
	101	0.15	0.94	1	2	20
	102	0.20	0.99	---	3	32
①	103	0.25	1.04	3	5	32
	104	0.30	1.09	18	15	12
	105	0.35	1.14	15	9	2
	106	0.40	1.19	6	12	1
②	107	0.45	1.24	3	---	---
	108	0.50	1.29	---	2	---
	109	0.55	1.34	1	---	---
③	110	0.60	1.39	---	---	---
			Total	47	48	99

Table 81: Lot wise distribution of material from Trial Trench (R2)

Layer	Lot No	Depth (from surface in m.)	Level (from datum point in m.)	Lithic Material		
				Flake	Crescent	Axe
①	501	0.5	1.32	3	--	1
	502	0.10	1.37	1	--	--
②	503	0.15	1.42	--	1	--
	504	0.20	1.47	--	--	--
		TOTAL		4	1	1

Table 82: Typological distribution of lithic and ceramic from Trial Trench – R1 (2 x 2 m.)

Sl.No	Typology	Numbers	Percentage
1	Flakes	47	24.22%
2	Chips	48	24.74%
3	Potsherds	99	51.03%
	TOTAL	194	99.99%

Table 83: Typological distribution of lithic from Trial Trench – R2 (1 x 1 m.)

Sl.No	Typology	Numbers	Percentage
1	Flakes	4	66.66%
2	Axe	1	16.66%
3	Crescent	1	16.66%
	TOTAL	6	99.98%

According to the above table 4 flake, 1 crescent and 1 axe have been collected from Trial Trench R2.

CERAMICS :

Ceramic analysis had developed into a specialized aspect of archaeology. Pottery probably provided the single most important yardstick for measuring technological and stylistic development. The analysis of shape both the overall vessel shape and the details of pottery analysis, through the shape analysis one can follows the sequential development and evolution of an object type. The body is the principal part of the pottery, as distinguished from the base, neck, rim and handle. The body shape can be definitely represented if the analyst can measure the complete pottery or at least one complete side.

So far as, concern trial trench at Telkoi, some potsherds have unearthed which are basically body sherds and rim sherds of red ware. Potsherds are having a medium to coarse fabric, heavily weathered and small in size.

Table 84: Physical analysis of soil sample Trial Trench-R1

Soil Sample No	Colour	Consolidated	Unconsolidated
1	Yellowish brown	Wet and dry	dry condition
2	Reddish	”	”
3	Reddish	Wet condition	-
4	”	”	”
5	”	”	”
6	”	”	”
7	”	”	”
8	”	”	”
9	”	”	”
10	Yellowish brown	”	”

The above table is analysed the physical condition of soil sample collected from every lot of excavated depth from the trial trench R1. The colour is ranged between reddish to yellowish brown. The soil samples are consolidated only in wet condition.

Table 85: Chemical analysis of soil sample Trial Trench - R1

Lot No	Layer	HCL	PH		
		Nil High Medium Low	Colour	No	
101		-	Slightly acidic	6.0	CH1
102		-	Slightly acidic	6.0	CH1
103	(1)	-	Slightly acidic	6.0	CH1
104		-	neutral	7.0	CH2
105		-	neutral	7.0	CH2

106		-	Strongly acidic	5.0	CH1
107	(2)	-	Slightly acidic	6.0	CH1
108		-	neutral	7.0	CH2
109		-	neutral	7.0	CH2
110	(3)	-	Slightly acidic	6.0	CH1

According to the above table, there is no reaction from these soil samples collected from Telkoi trial trench excavation. By PH test it is decided that out of 10 samples 4 are neutral, 5 are slightly acidic and one is strongly acidic in nature.

Table 86: Lot-wise Pedological analysis of soil Trial Trench- R1 (2 x 2 m.)

Lot No.	Depth	Level	Sieve size				Remark
	From surface (in m.)	Datum point (in m.)	2 mm	0.2 mm	0.6 mm	Residue	
101	0.15	0.94	1g	2.5g	0.5g	6g	10% Coarse sand, 25% fine sand, 5% silt & 60% clay
102	0.20	0.99	1.2g	1g	0.8g	7g	12% Coarse sand, 10% fine sand, 8% silt & 70% clay
103	0.25	1.04	0g	2g	0.8g	7.2g	0% Coarse sand, 20% fine sand, 8% silt & 72% clay
104	0.30	1.09	0g	2g	1g	7g	0% Coarse sand, 20% fine sand, 10% silt & 70% clay

105	0.35	1.14	0g	1.5g	1.2g	7.3g	0% Coarse sand, 15% fine sand, 12% silt & 73% clay
106	0.40	1.19	0g	1.5g	1.5g	7g	0% Coarse sand, 15% fine sand, 15% silt & 70% clay
107	0.45	1.24	0g	1.5g	0.7g	7.8g	0% Coarse sand, 15% fine sand, 7% silt & 78% clay
108	0.50	1.29	0g	1.2g	0.8g	8g	0% Coarse sand, 12% fine sand, 8% silt & 80% clay
109	0.55	1.34	0g	1.2g	0.8g	8g	0% Coarse sand, 12% fine sand, 8% silt & 80% clay
110	0.60	1.39	0g	1g	1g	8g	0% Coarse sand, 10% fine sand, 10% silt & 80% clay

SECTION DRAWING

Section is the mirror of trench. The section is a scale measured drawing of the vertical profile (strata) of the site, including the inter-relationship of soils, trench walls, bulks and architectural features. To establishing its relationship to the original ground level of the ground surface, draw in the datum line on the section drawing.

In the Telkoi trial excavation, the section drawing of trial trench R1 represents the deposit of Humus, Layer 1, Layer 2 and Layer 3 respectively 4 cm, 32 cm, 48 cm, and 60 cm. from surface of the trench.

ANALYSIS OF HISTORICAL ARTEFACTS

Besides the prehistoric evidences, the Telkoi region has witnessed very few historical artefacts which include potsherds, iron slags and rubber stone. The historic site of Telkoi is located on the left bank of the river Somakoi, about 500 m south-west of the neolithic site of Telkoi where a seasonal stream is flowing in the eastern and joints the river Somakoi in the north-eastern part of the mound. The mound is covered an area about 150 x 100 sq.m. Extensive agricultural fields and modern settlements are present across the river. The total height of the mound is about six meter from the existing water level of the stream. The mound is undisturbed and is scattered with a large quantity of potsherds, a dimple scarred rubber stone, and flake of deprival dolerite. The site has also witnessed a large quantity of iron slags in the west of the site across the stream about a distance of 500 m. It is important to mention here that a few fragmented brunt bricks have also been noticed at the site. A flat quartzite piece of 30 x 14 x 10 cm having polishing impressions is also noticed at the site.

Potsherds:

1. (TK-10) Rim fragment of a red ware, pot with wide orifice, out turned rounded rim, fine to medium fabric.
2. (TK-22) Rim fragment of a black ware, pot, wide orifice, out turned slightly triangular rim with gray core, constricted neck, fine to medium fabric.
3. (TK-V) Rim fragment of a black ware, big sized pot with wide orifice, beaked rim with constricted neck, two regular incised marks on sloping shoulder, grey, core, fine to medium fabric.
4. (TK-IV) Rim fragment of a red ware, storage jar, out turned beaded rim with constricted neck, possible oval shaped body, wide orifice, medium to coarse fabric.
5. (TK-II) Rim fragment of a black ware, carinated deep bowl, everted rim, grey core, fine to medium fabric.
6. (TK-20) Rim fragment of a red ware, storage jar, inturned beaked rim with finger punching designs, wide orifice, medium fabric.

7. (TK-8) Rim fragment of a black ware, pot, everted rim with constricted neck, grey core, fine to medium fabric.
8. (TK-VI) same as above, but one regular incised mark is noticed on sloping shoulder.
9. (TK-19) Rim fragment of a black ware, storage jar, bilateral projecting rim, medium fabric.
10. (TK-12) Rim fragment of a black ware, storage jar, inturned bilateral projecting rim with grey core, medium orifice, fine to medium fabric.
11. (TK-I) Rim fragment of a red ware, pot, out turned flaring rim, short concave neck, fine fabric.
12. (TK-III) Rim fragment of red ware, storage jar, neck less slightly out turned rounded rim, grey with fine fabric.
13. (TK-32) Rim fragment of a red ware, storage jar, inturned rounded rim, small orifice, medium fabric.
14. (TK-28) Rim fragment of a black ware, pot, short beaked rim, small orifice, medium fabric.
15. (TK-9) Rim fragment of a red ware, lid, legged rim, fine to medium fabric.
16. (TK-7) Rim fragment of a black ware, lid, treatment of black colour on upper surface, grey inner core, ledged rim, fine to medium fabric.
17. (TK-IX) Rim fragment of a red ware, flat based deep bowl with sharpened rim, medium fabric.
18. (TK-14) Bodysherd of a red ware, two regular incised marks present just above the carination on bodysherd, medium fabric.
19. (TK-29) Bodysherd of black ware, medium fabric.
20. (TK-18) Bodysherd of a red ware, carinated, two regular incised marks present just below the carination, medium to coarse fabric.
21. (TK-OX) Spout of a red ware, medium fabric, possible used for spouted medium sized pot (lota type).
22. (TK-24) Base of a red ware, flat base, medium to coarse fabric.

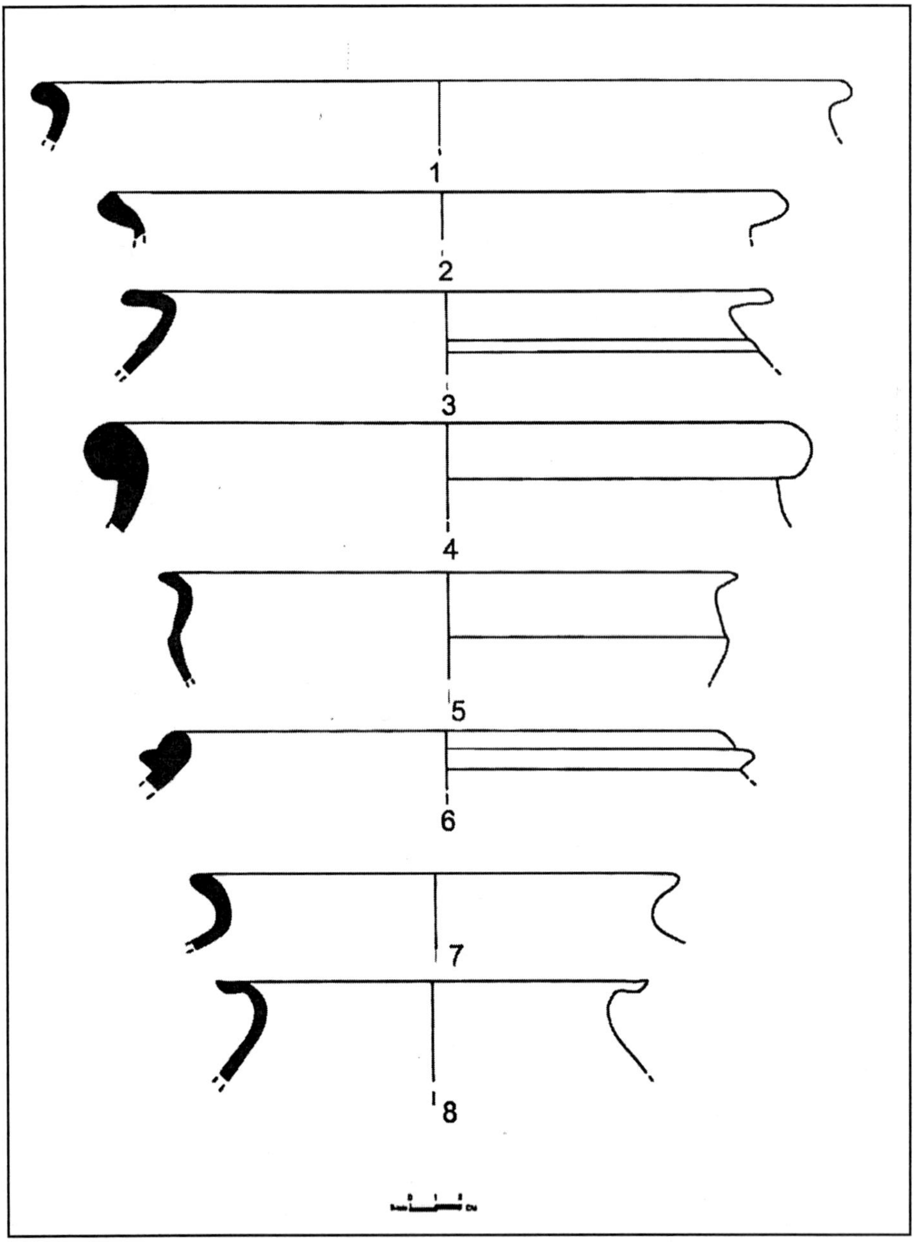

Fig-27: Historical period pottery from Telkoi.

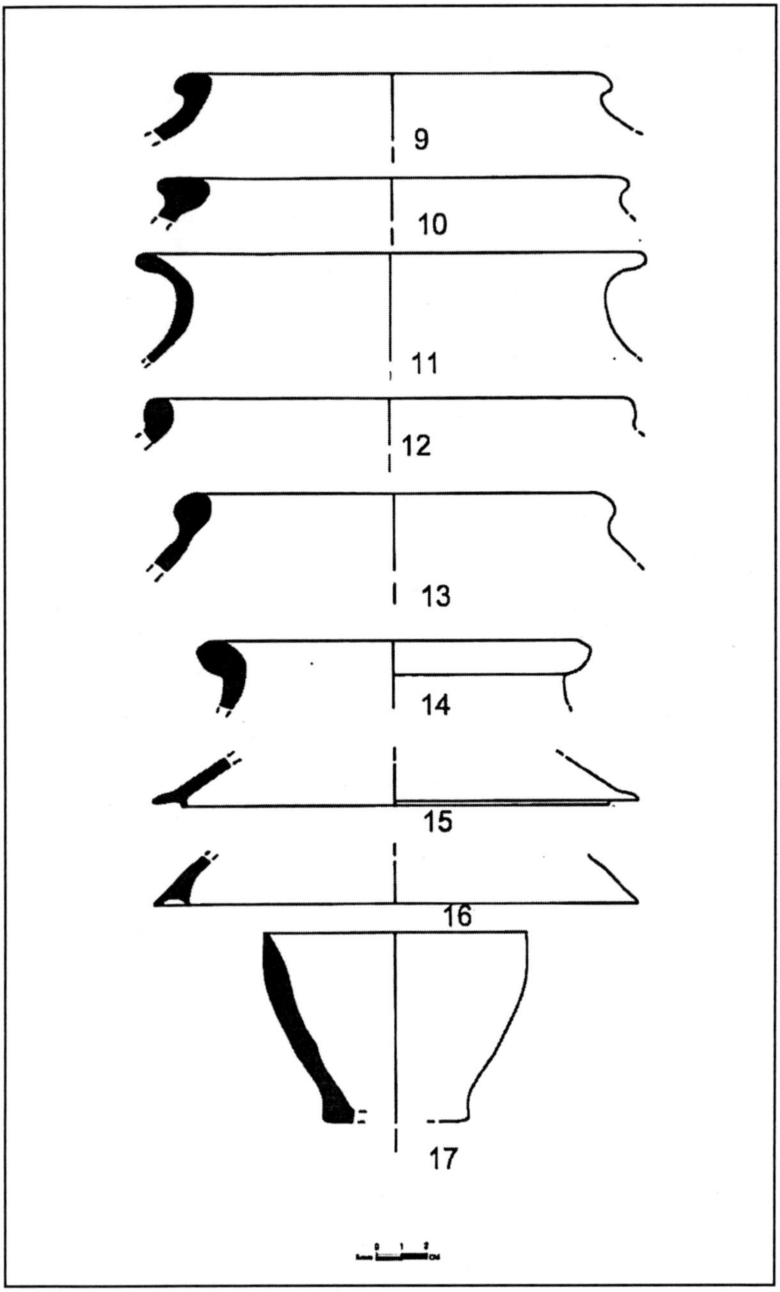

Fig-28: Historical period pottery from Telkoi.

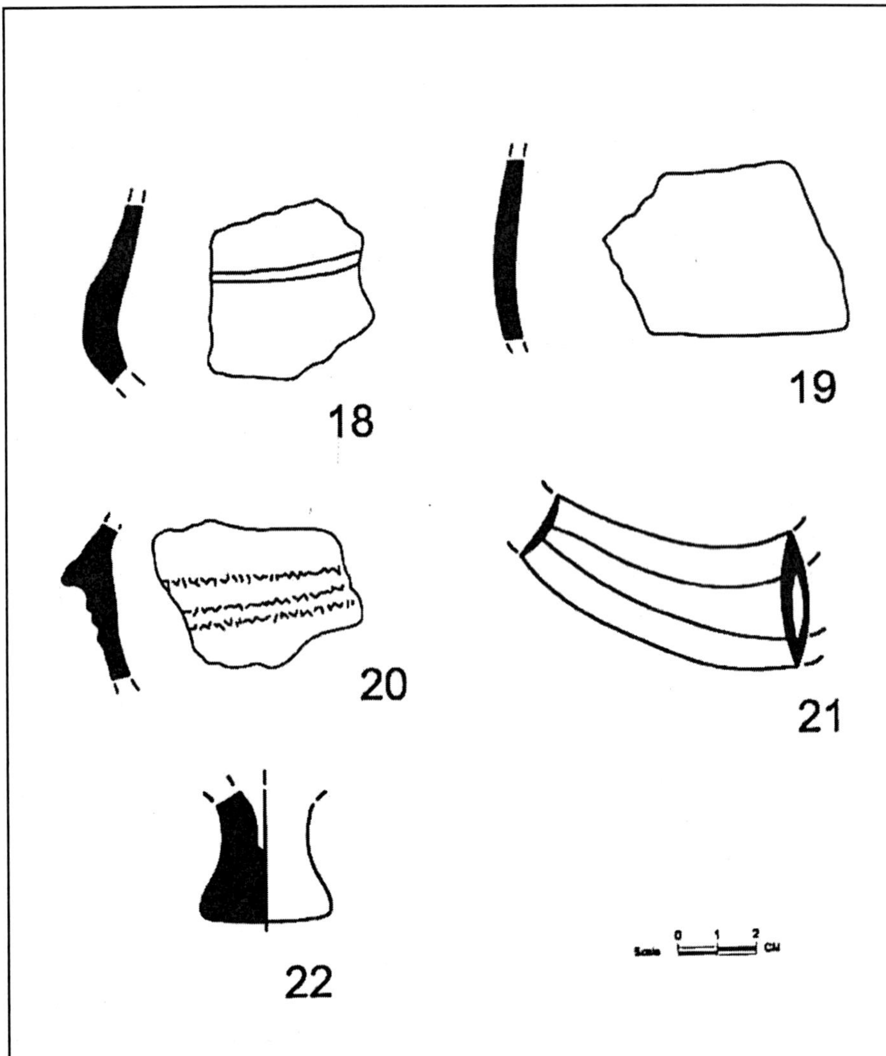

Fig-29: Historical period pottery from Telkoi.

Main features of the Trial Trench Excavation and Historical sites of Somakoi Basin

From the intensive exploration along with the Somakoi Basin specifically the Telkoi area of Keonjhar district, is revealed that this geographical region has much potential of prehistoric culture especially mesolithic and neolithic culture. The intensive survey in both side of river in and around Telkoi has resulted 12 prehistoric and one historical site. On the basis of discovery the Telkoi prehistoric site has been selected for the trial excavation. Hence from the trial excavation a good number of flake and chips of the neolithic culture have been collected. The following important characteristic features of trial excavation and historical site are inferred from present survey.

1. On the basis of distribution the Telkoi site has been selected for trial excavation, hence the two artefacts concentration zone i.e R1 (2 x 2 m.) and R2 (1 x 1 m.) selected for trial excavations.
2. Ceramics is a good index of cultural continuity and change. There is very meager pottery in neolithic period in Odisha. However, the study has yielded a small amount of ceramics in fragile in nature with neolithic flake from trial excavation at Telkoi imply that ceramics used in neolithic period in the North Odisha.
3. The deposits of neolithic flake, chips along with semi finished axe upto the depth 1.39 m. in the trial trench implies that manufacturing area of neolithic period.
4. Analysis of soil sample from the trial trenches reflect more than 70% clay and slightly acidic in nature.
5. The finding of microlith beneath the neolithic deposits reflects the cultural succession of the region.
6. The only historical site recovered a good amount of potsherds. It is also noticed iron slag and brick bats at the site.

CHAPTER 5

GENERAL OBSERVATION AND CONCLUSION

Although the lithic tradition in India has started as early as the Lower Palaeolithic period with heavy component tools and its continuation process its change in technologically and in material use also. To explore the Somakoi river basin, i.e Somakoi of this region in general and Katarapalli to Nuagarh revenue village area in particular. Approximately 7 sq km. was surveyed on the Somakoi basin around Telkoi. The river Somakoi originates in Keonjhar district and it is flowing through the hilly regions of both Keonjhar and Angul district.

Apart from one historical site, 12 sites of prehistoric nature were explored in this region and out of which 5 sites are from Unit-II, 5 sites from Unit-III and 2 sites from Unit-IV. On the basis of river bank locations, 8 sites are from left bank and 4 sites from the right bank. The left bank is important for our study because the sites are more implementiferous and some sections are visible on this bank locations. One trial trench excavation has been done in the left bank of Somakoi in Telkoi. The importance of the site is (a) from the site ground artefacts such as axe and flakes are found, (b) finding of microliths beneath the neolithic deposits and (c) potsherds of red ware are found in weathered condition.

INTER-RELATIONSHIP BETWEEN SITES

All the 12 sites explored are divided into four units on the basis of clockwise on Topo-map. All the sites are named after the name of the nearby village. The distance of the village and the site range are between 1 to 1 ½ km, the every unit cover 3 ½ sq. km on the Topo-map. Approximately 7 kilometres area has been studied in this present work.

In Unit-I, 2 ½ sq. km. area has been surveyed starting from Telkoi, but there was no lithic remain found. Unit-II extension is 3 ½ sq km., from where five implementiferous site has been discovered. These sites are Tungur pahar, Kadalikund, Balisahi, Danduamunda and Kotarapali. The Unit- III has recorded five sites such as College area (400 x 300 m.), Madhusudanpur lacality-1 (500 x 500 m.), Madhusudanpur locality- 2 (200 x 100 m.), Madhusudanpur locality-3 (200 x 200 m.), and the extension of Gundurijhora site is 100 x 100 m. The Unit-IV has reported the Telkoi (excavated site) site is 300 x 200 m. and Nuagarh site having 200 x 100 m. However, the sites of Unit-II and Unit-III are more extended than the Unit-IV.

Evidence of lithic cultures from Unit-II area.

There are five sites in the Unit-II. They are Tungur Pahar, Kadalikund, Balisahi, Danduamunda and Katarapali. All sites are studied on the basis of surface recovery. On the basis of recovery of artefacts typology and cultural segments, the sites have been interpreted. The details have been presented below.

Lower Palaeolithic: In the site at Tungur Pahar 2 lower palaeolithic tool have been collected. The dominant typologies are chopper 1 (50 %) and hand axe 1 (50 %). From the site at Kadalikund 11 lower palaeolithic tools have been collected. The significant typology are hand axe 6 (54.54%), cleaver 3 (27.27 %) and chopper 2 (18.18 %).The dominant type is hand axe.

Mesolithic: The site of Tungur Pahar has yielded a good number of microlith typologies, which include fluted core 10 (47.61 %), flakes 5 (23.80 %), blades 5 (23.80 %) and borer 1 (4.76 %). In the site at Balisahi, 68 microliths have been collected. Here the dominant typologies are blade 31 (45.58 %), fluted core 9 (13.23 %) and flake 10 (14.70 %), whereas other are scraper, point, notch, borer 18 (26.46 %). The dominant variety is blade.

Neolithic : The site at Tungur Pahar has evidenced 18 neoliths artefacts. The significant type is flake 8 (44.44 %), ring stone 3 (16.66 %), hammer stone 2 (11.11%), quern 1 (5.55 %), polisher 1 (5.55 %) and blank 3 (16.66 %). The site at Balisahi has yielded 19 neoliths with predominant of flake 9 (47.36 %), axe 4 (21.05 %) and other are chisel, ring stone, cobble 6 (31.56 %). Similarly the sites at Danduamunda 2 neolithic flakes have been found. In the site at Katarapali, 5 neoliths including 3 ring stone, 1 flake and 1 rubber stone. The site at Kadalikund has yielded 5 neoliths with predominance of blank 2 (40%), flake 1 (20%), chisel 1 (20%) and polisher 1 (20%).

Evidence of lithic cultures from Unit-III area

There are five explored sites on the Unit-III of the Telkoi survey area. They are Madhusudanpur locality-1, Madhusudanpur locality-2, Madhusudanpur locality-3, College area and Gurdurijhora. All these sites are surveyed by intensive exploration. The sites are studied and their cultural sequences are divided on the basis of findings of palaeo-relics from the surface.

Lower Palaeolithic: Out of 5 sites, 3 sites of Unit-II has yielded Lower Palaeolithic tools. The Madhusudanpur locality-1 site has been reported 4 lower Palaeolithic tool. The significant typologies are hand axe 3 (75%) and cleaver 1 (25 %). From the Madhusudanpur locality-3, one hand axe has been reported. The site at College area has 2 lower palaeoliths including one hand axe and one chopper revealed. But the other two sites at Madhusudanpur locality-2 and Gundurijhara did not reveal any lower palaeolithic tools.

Upper Palaeolithic : From the site at Madhusudanpur locality-3, 11 Upper Palaeolithic tools have been collected. The major typologies are flake 4 (36.36%), scraper 4 (36.36%), blade 2 (18.18%) and nodule 1 (9.09%). In the other sites of Telkoi survey does not reveal any recoveries of Upper Palaeolithic tool.

Mesolithic : The site at Madhusudanpur locality-1 has revealed 3 microliths including 2 fluted core and 1 scraper. Madhusudanpur locality-2 site has yielded 11 microliths, out of which significant typologies are flake 4 (36.36 %), scraper 4 (36.36 %), fluted core 1 (9.09%), and blade 2 (18.18%). The site at Madhusudanpur locality-3 has yielded 57 microliths. The important typologies are fluted core 23 (40.3 %), blade 15 (26.31%) and scraper 10 (17.54%), other are flake, borer, point, 9 (15.77%). From the site at College area, 114 microliths have been collected. Here the dominant typologies are fluted core 21 (18.42%), flake 17 (14.91 %), blade 44 (38.59 %) and scraper 13 (14.91%) and other typologies are point, burin, borer and awl. The dominant variety is blade. The Gundurijhora site has not revealed any microliths.

Neolithic : The site of Madhusudanpur locality-1 has yielded 4 neoliths, which includes 2 blank and 2 axe. Similarly, the site at Madhusudanpur locality-2 has recovered 6 neoliths including 2 blank, 2 flake and 2 axe. The site at Madhusudanpur locality-3 has yielded 37 neoliths with predominance of flake 14 (37.83%), ring stone 7 (18.91%), blank 5 (13.51%), chisel 4 (10.81%), axe 4 (10.81%), hammer stone 2 (5.40%) and rubber stone 3 (8.10%). The site of College area has reported 36 neoliths, which includes ring stone 17 (47.22%), hammer stone 5 (13.88%), rubber stone 2 (5.55%), axe 3 (8.33%), flake 6 (16.66%), blank 1 (2.77%) and chisel 2 (5.55%).

Evidence of lithic cultures from Unit-IV area

On the Unit-IV, the two sites Telkoi (excavated site) and Nuagarh have been discovered on the left bank of the river Somakoi. In addition to surface collection a trial excavation was taken at Telkoi site to understand the cultural deposit. On the basis of recovery of artefacts, typology and cultural segments of the sites have been interpreted. The details are as given as below.

Lower Palacolithic : The site at Telkoi has yielded 2 lower palaeolithic flake by intensive exploration. Similarly, the site at Nuagarh has reported 2 lower palaeolithic flakes.

Mesolithic : The site at Telkoi has yielded 8 microliths, the dominant typologies are scraper 4 (50%), fluted core 2 (25%), flake 1 (12.5%) and blade 1 (12.5%). From the site at Nuagarh evidenced 5 microliths. The significant typologies are scraper 2 (40%), fluted core 1, flake 1 and blade 1.

Neoliths : The site of Telkoi has yielded a good number of neolithic artefacts from the surface. 85 neolithic artefacts have been collected from this site. The significant typologies are flake 42 (49.41%), chips 42 (49.41%) and axe 1 (1.17%). The site at Nuagarh also evidenced 4 neolithic artefacts with predominant of polisher 2 (50%), chisel 1 (25%) and ring stone 1 (25%).

Trial excavation relationship with Grid (surface) data

The purpose is to establish a relationship between the surface data and the data collected from Telkoi grid for understanding the site in great detail. From the grid at Telkoi, the data were collected out of a grid measuring 5 x 5 m. The contents are registered as follows; flakes, chips and axe. There are 29 flakes which have been recovered from A1, A3, B2, B3, B4, B5, C1, C2, C3, D1, D2, D3, D4, D5, E5, Similarly 31 number of chips were collected from A1, A2 A3, A5, B1, B2, B4, B5, C1, C2, D4, D5, E1, E2 and E3, one chipped bar axe collected from D4.

After undertaking a surface survey in specific localities, it was intended to observe the nature concentration of different stone tool typologies. On the basis of the concentration it was speculated that, in case of excavation similar typological evidences may be found with specific stratigraphic details. Therefore, two trial trenches were taken into consideration at Telkoi to know their stratification and cultural deposits, if any.

Near at Telkoi grid, a trial trench R1, measuring 2 x 2 m. was excavated. The excavation continued upto 0.60 m. depth. From the trench got a broad picture about deposition of artefacts relics such as 47 neolithic flake, 48 neolithic chips and 99 potsherds have been recovered. 47 neolithic flakes have been recovered from Lot No.101, Lot No.103 to Lot No.107 and Lot No.109. Besides the lithics, 99 potsherds have been recovered from this trench R1 in the Lot No.101 to Lot No.106.

Second trench, designated as Trench R2 and measuring 1 x 1m. was excavated, near to the trench R1. The excavation continued up to the 0.32m. depth. The lithic contains are registered as neolithic flake, axe and crescent. There are six numbers of artefacts which have been recovered from this excavation. Out of these, 4 flake from lot No. 501 and Lot No. 502, 1 axe from Lot No. 501, and 1 crescent from Lot No. 503 were collected.

It may be concluded from the study that the distribution of prehistoric artefacts on the surface may bear some relationship with the relics recorded from the excavation. The materials collected out of the excavation are geo-chronologically significant. It is difficult to interpret their other aspects but the materials of the excavation explain the significance of stratification which may be further explained in terms of a cultural chronology in the area under survey.

COMPARISON WITH SURROUNDING AREAS OF ODISHA

An attempt has been made to present a comparative picture relating to Palaeolithic, Mesolithic and Neolithic cultures distributed in surrounding regions of northern Odisha. The cultural data of the area under survey around Telkoi are to be compared with the surrounding cultural data of West Bengal and Jharkhand in general and Mayurbhanj, Keonjhar, Angul and Sundargarh in particular.

The district of West Singhbhum is situated to the south and south-west of Ranchi district and occupied the south-eastern end of Chotanagpur plateau is close to the district Keonjhar of Odisha. Geologically the district consists of pre-cenozoic metamorphic and igneous rocks as well as the deposits of tertiary age comprised of grits and gravels, which are largely confined to the eastern Singhbhum (Ghosh 1970). The discovery of tools implements sites or area containing palaeolithic, mesolithic and neolithic implements including pottery and other objects in the district have been made from the Ghatsila area located in the main Subarnarekha valley (Mitra 1929).The discovery of prehistoric implements from the Jamshedpur area had been made by E.F.O Murray while he was engaged in surveying the ancient copper mining in the locality. Further S.C Roy reported microlithic tools of the mesolithic age from Jamshedpur town (IAR 1959-60). In the neolithic typology the wedge shaped axe and shouldered celt were found in the field near the bank of Subarnarekha river by V. Ball in 1875. Similarly S.C Sinha survey the Chandil area especially the north of confluence area of Kharkhai with Subarnarekha river (Sinha 1951). The Sini area near Sanjay valley extensively surveyed by D. Sen and A.K Ghosh located sites and reported lower palaeolithic, middle palaeolithic, upper palaeolithic, microliths of mesolithic age and neolithic implements from Barudih, Dugni and Ukri sites (Sen 1969).

The first discovery of microliths consisting of chert flakes and knives in the Chakradharpur and Chaibasa of West Singhbhum district had been made by Captain Beeching (Beeching 1868). The tools were found either laying loose in the gravels or in sandy depression. C.W Anderson had discovered prehistoric stone implements in the valley of Sanjay and its tributaries of Chakradharpur (Anderson 1917). In Roro river, a tributary to Kharkhai was initially survey by Calcutta University observed section along Tilimdah site and reported lower palaeolithic tool types such as hand axe, clevers had been obtained from the lower gravel conglomerate, while one or two scraper of the middle palaeolithic had been recovered from the upper gravels (Sen and Ghosh 1960). Similarly the Jamda-Goa region south west singhbhum close to the present study area had been reported middle Palaeolithic implements from the Karo river on upper gravel level (Ghosh 1970).

The Barda bridge collection artefacts have been divided into two groups as (i) the finished implements and (ii) by-products. The finished implements have been made out of flake –blades and appropriate cores. The blades with the parallel sides are roughly rectangular in form, few characterised with very little secondary retouch through pronounced medial or truncated ridge (Sen and Chaturvedi 1957).

The excavation at Lotapahad by S.R Roy of Government of Bihar (1966-67), retrieved lower Palaeolithic and upper Palaeolithic artefacts in period I and period II by the occurrence of microliths of both geometric and non geometric variety (IAR 1966-67).

In Jharkhand, the first neolithic tools were discovered in the Singhbhum district by Captain Beaching in the year 1868 (Beaching 1868). Anderson encounter with neolithic implements in the valley of Sanjay and its tributary stream especially two miles west of Lotapahad to Sini towards north-east in the district of Singhbhum (Anderson 1917). The discovery of a few polished stone hammers from Nadup or Ladup about 5 mile and half east of the workings of the cape copper mine at Matigara in Singhbhum district (Biswas 1918, Raychaudhury. 1985). In 1952, R.C. Kar discovered a neolithic site at Haribera on the bank of Kharkhai, a tributary to Sanjay river in Singhbhum district. The important findings are chisel of extreme large size charecterised by chipping and partially smoothing (Krishnaswami 1953). The collection of pre historic potsherds from Barda and Bongara has technically studied by G.S Ray and provides some significant elements of the ceramics industry. The potsherds are of mainly represented by a crude and hand made. It is interesting to note that both site potsherds were associated with neolithic industry (Roy and Ray 1963).

Similar to Chhotanagpur plateau of Jharkhand and Odisha, the west Bengal has also yielded potential archaeological evidences, principally the geographical setting of the southern region of West Bengal had offer possibilities and also limitations for prehistoric study. Evidence of the prehistoric culture of West Bengal has been reported from the south-western part of the state, which covered by vast stretched of undulating land and drainage system and are about 300 mesolithic sites have been reported so far from the lateritic uplands.

The site at Birbhanpur in Bardhaman district of West Bengal exposed the flake tool industry, the tool types are comprised of blades, points, scrapers, lunates, borers and burins. The mesolithic site at

Paluldanga in Birbhum district has reported microliths on the eroded lateritic surface. The mesolithic phase has been divided into phase-I and Phase-II on the basis of stratigraphy (Chakrabarti, Bhatacharya and Chakrabarti 1982). Another important Mesolithic site was located at Chamargora in Medinapur district. Here Mesolithic artefacts consist of microliths and quite similar with Mesolithic I of Paruldanga.

Lalgarh in Medinapur district is an important neolithic site, situated about 5 km south of Bamal in the Kangsavati river valley has reported few elongated Neolithic celts from surface level whereas from trial digging has been unearthed stone implements including ground stone celts and chisel. In Tarapheni river valley has witnessed Neolithic site like Bamandihi, Kechanda, Bhulabeda, Orgonda, Dumurkonda, Laljal etc. These sites have yielded microliths and neoliths. Similarly the Silavati river valley Neolithic has found from Bagridihi such as four finely smoothed barcelt (Chakravarty M 1967).

In Bankura district, from the Damodar river valley at Bon Asuria several Neolithic barcelts and few stone celts have been recovered (Dasgupta 1966). The site at Kankradara and its adjucent areas have yielded a developed achulian industry besides neolithic. Neolithic celt, pounder, ring stone are picked up as surface finds (Chakravarty 1967). The Susania hill excavation reveals cultural assemblage of neolithic to iron using culture people. Along with the artefacts of bone and antler, lithic tools particular burin, hand drill, blade and scrapers have also been found. Bone implements include harpoon, spear head etc. (Pal 1996).

The discovery of neolithic implements from Singhbhum (Jharkhand) have comprises the tool types of chisels, rounded butt are faceted tools and bar chisels. The main neolithic tool types of Bengal are ring stone, shouldered celts, triangular axes and axe with rounded butt are significant one.

Surface collection have been made form a quite few sites in the districts of Mayurbhanj, Keonjhar, Angul and Sundargarh in Odisha. Paramananda Acharya reported neolithic artefacts from his native village Baidypur in Mayurbhanj, northern Orissa and in the late thirties reported Kuliana along with E.C. Worman, a Harvard University researcher. Later the site was excavated by the Calcutta University under the direction of N.K. Bose and D. Sen (1948). It is important to note here that Kuliana is the first excavated lower Palaeolithic site in India.The Kuchai site was excavated by Thapar and reported bar axe, chisel and rounded butt axes (Thaper 1958). Kuchai (Mayurbhanj) the only excavated site from where microliths are associated with pottery found from lower level. The microliths tools are included blade, pointed flakes, crescents and prismatic cores. Further the site was yielded neolithic tool types such as chisels, pounders, mace heads and grinding stones from the upper levels and pottery with ground stores are recovered from the surface exploration.

Recent work of Mahanta in the Mayurbhanj and Keonjhar districts of Northern Odisha is revealed that this geographical region has much potential for the evidence of neolithic culture. The intensive micro area survey in and around Rairangpur, Baripada, Jashipur, Karanjia, Dhenkikot and Telkoi areas has resulted the discovery of 39 neolithic sites. With view to the geomorphological location, these sites have been classified into three broad types, viz. the foothill sites, the piedmont sites and the river bank sites. Hence, from the survey, numerous finished and semi-finished artefacts of the neolithic culture have been collected for analytical study. Jashipur area in Mayurbhanj was surveyed by Mahanta for fulfilling his M.A. assignment and found some prehistoric sites of different periods (Mohanta 1998). Further he surveyed Manda region of river Bhatchatra, Andhari and Khadkai and brought to light three sites (Mahanta 1992-93). A field work jointly carried out by Mahanta and Behera in some of the river valleys of Bamanghaty area and discovered several new mesolithic sites and documented the lithic implement by taking all the technical aspect of the physical description (Mohanta and Behera 2007).

K.K. Basa of Department of Anthropology, Utkal University in his M.A. dissertation on "Paleohistory of Mayurbhanj" has reported new Palaeolithic sites. Further he again started exploration in river basins of Burhabalanga, Subamarekha, Khadkai and Deo and brought to light many new prehistoric sites (Basa 1984).

In the basin of the river Chipat, a tributary river of Burhabalanga was reported different prehistoric sites by Department of Anthropology, Utkal University. A trial excavation at a site called Chelinendi near Kuchai was under taken for systematic recording of the antiquities and recorded pebbles, quartzite, burnt clay, chips, potsherds and tools (Sahoo 1986).

The Deo river basin around Karanjia was surveyed by B. Khillar and collected prehistoric implements belong to Palaeolithic to Neolithic period.

In recent years, most comprehensive work on Mayurbhanj prehistory has been carried out by S. Chakrabarty. He surveyed the river Baitarani around Khiching and Similipal massif and reported prehistoric sites belong to Palaeolithic to Neolithic period in both secondary and primary context (Chakrabarty 2000).

Mohapatra's pioneering work mostly exploratory in nature and restricted to Central and Northern Odisha. His systematic research on prehistoric sites was includes the river valleys of Brahmani, Burhabalanga and Mahanadi of Odisha. He studied the stratigraphy of the river valley in relation to the prehistoric assemblages and established regional sequences. He went on to make a comparison with corresponding industries elsewhere in India which were both interesting and useful (Mohapatra 1958-59).

From Keonjhar, Mohanty's intensive exploration under taken in the Champua, Ghosipura, Ghatgaon, Palaspal, Harichandanpur, and Patana tehsils and reported 58 Measolithic site. Most of sites are primary in nature and reported microlith include blade, pointed flakes, crescent, scraper with heavy implements assemblages. The microlithic from these sites compare well with one another in term of both raw material and typological features. A well developed blade technology is the most out standing feature of the keonjhar microlithic assemblages.The heavy implements had been shophisticated worked out and dolerite was the principle raw material used for manufacturing (Mohanty 1998).

Pallahara, a small town is located bank of Mankara river a tributary of river Brahmani and its vicinity were surveyed intensively and resulted artefacts belonging to Palaeolithic, Mesolithic and Neolithic Cultures. A trial trench measuring 1 x1 mt. was exposed in Bajpur with 53 lithic artefacts belonging to the mesolithic and neolithic. Neolithic artefacts were recovered from first two layer and consisted of flakes, chips and no finished tool where as microliths from last layer represented bladelets, blade and crescents made on chert. The pottery from Bajpur excavation was made on slow wheel and few show coil method being also used. Two main types of pottery are identified i.e coarse red were and black and red ware. The other sites of this area were recovered 205 neolithic artefacts and the main tool types of the neolithic here are axe, chisel, dimple-scarred rubber, flakes and chips. The axes were usually made with rectangular butt, but a few are also found with irregular butt. Their working edge are bevelled and made sharp ended. Chisels both finished and unfinished along with blank of quadrilateral shape are found. The dimple scarred rubber with depression dimple like shallow marks on one side or both side. The neolithic raw material is available abundantly in locally and predominantly dolorite (Basa 2000).

The Banaigarh region comes under the northeastern hill regions of Odisha highland and falls in Sundargarh district. The area was extensively surveyed in the year 1985-88 which resulted in the discovery of a large number of celt manufacturing sites. Few sites of this locality are associated with celts and ceramics. Most of the sites are open air site in nature and have been found in two different geographical context viz. Sites on the alluvial surface of the river banks and those in the foot hill or piedmont area. Behera has identified two types of sites i.e workshop sites and habitational sites with celt and ceramics. The workshop sites are further divided into minor workshop sites and major workshop sites. The minor sites are believed to be used for a short duration where as major work shop sites represent with form of massive debris mounds. From these sites mainly finished and semi finished celt of different types along with pebble tools, axes, adze, chopper-chopping, bored–stone, spear head, grain pounders, elongated knife etc. The raw material dolerite is predominantly used for manufacturing artefacts. The excavation at Bonaigarh neolithic cultural complex belonged to pre iron phase and was associated with a coarse gritty-tempered red ware (Behera 2000).

In comparison to North Odisha, the lithic cultures of south western Odisha appear to be late in occurrence. The mesolithic cultural sequence in this area is more widely and profusely distributed around the rivers of Tel, Ong, Sengodi, Sndal and Jira (Tripathy 1969-72). The industry is mostly non-geometric in nature. The glimpse of neolithic is evidenced by the recovery of miniature celts and mace heads.

In Kantala region of Angul district, explored by the department of Anthropology, Utkal University has reported few sites, from which microlithic and neolithic tool have been collected. Microlithic includes blade, flake, scraper, borer, fluted core and neolithic remains are celt, axe, chisel and ring stone. It is necessary to compare the lithic materials and potsherd of the site with the nearby reported (Trial excavated) neolithic site Kamparkala (Mishra 1997). Most of the lithic materials of Kamparkala site are mainly neolithic culture, whereas palaeolithic and microlithic artefacts are least in number. These ground stone implements are made out of fine grained granite. The ground stone implements are like axe, chisel, ring stone etc. recovered from Kamparkala and its surrounding eight sites. The Kamparkala excavated potsherds were basically course red ware and black and red ware. It is also noteworthy to mention here that Kamparkala site is very rich in the sense of prehistoric archaeology (Dehuri 1997). Further the present author has been reported more then 30 sites in the Khakharua valley and reported microlithic tools like blade, flake, scraper, borer, fluted core and neolithic remains are bar celt, celt, axe, chisel and ring stone (Dehuri 2019).

The recent reported sites around Telkoi may have some relationship with these prehistoric cultures of surrounding regions should have been compared with the cultures of Telkoi region. There are wide varieties of lower Palaeoliths, upper Palaeolithic, mesoliths and neoliths are found from the sites around Telkoi, A large number of flakes and blades are also collected from the College area, Madhusudanpur locality-3, Balisahi and Tungur Pahar sites. Besides other nine sites, the site Danduamunda, Katarapali and Gundurijhora have yielded only with the neoliths. The grid area documentation has evidenced the concentration of flakes and chips indicate a tool manufacturing site. The potsherds are also found from this area but they are too much fragmentary.

The new data provided through prehistoric survey in and around Somakoi basin of Telkoi region and trial excavation, the collected lithic remains are Palaeolithic, Mesolithic and Neolithic culture. It is noteworthy to mention that few potshards are also reported from the Telkoi site which is associated with Neolithic culture. The potsherds are very much fragmentary in nature, so it is difficult to distinguish its colour and fabric only. In both these two sites lithic remains and potsherds are the almost similar type.

SUMMARY AND CONCLUSION

An attempt has been made in this work to present brief information about the general observations made during this survey in and around Telkoi region of Somakoi Basin. It is difficult task to briefly present a summary of all those which have been discussed in the preceding chapters to deduce any conclusion. The results are based on the couple of two months November to January (1997-98) field work conducted around Telkoi localities in the district of Keonjhar. The present work contents the result of survey of prehistoric sites around Telkoi, the details of trial excavation and the physical and chemical analysis of the soils are collected from the section scraping of trial trenches.

The present work is presented in five chapters. In chapter-I include the short introduction of prehistoric research and about present environment of Odisha regarding the location of the district, the administrative background, topography, physiographic features, forest, hill, drainage system, geology, climate, rain fall and population. The river systems include the Baitarani and the Brahmani river system along with small streamlets. This is succeeded by the review of literature on the archaeological work of North and North Central Odisha.

Chapter-II includes the objective and method of survey, location of sites and analysis of the cultural materials of the Somakoi basin. The total survey area has been divided into four Unit, such as Unit-I, Unit-II, Unit -III & Unit- IV. The Chapter also contains descriptions of 12 sites discovered in the Somakoi basin from surface exploration and an account of the lithic materials of the area. The prime recoveries of this area are lower Palaeoliths, upper Palaeoliths, microliths of Mesolithic and Neoliths. Large number of Neoliths and Microliths are found almost all sites.

The detailed study has been presented in this chapter-III, it includes the data analysis, stratigraphy study, the details of the soil analysis collected from the sites, the lay out of grid and analysis of lithic implements recovered from the grid and metric analysis of the different cultural segments. It also contains an account detail of the lower Palaeolithic, upper Palaeolithic, Mesolithic and Neolithic recoveries from present survey in the Somakoi basin. With regard to the upper Palaeolithic culture, only one site (Madhusudanpur locality-3) has been found with 11 artefacts. Hence, it may be important evidence that the Somakoi basin had more sites that not encountered in the present survey. On the other hand, we come across seven sites with lower Palaeolithic, eight sites Mesolithic and 12 sites of Neolithic artefacts. This implies that during Palaeolithic, Mesolithic and Neolithic period, the Somakoi basin became an important destination of prehistoric man. The microlithic artefacts have been includes the types of scraper, blade, point, flake, backed blade, parallel sided blade, denticulate blade, double sided blade, borer, awl, burin, fluted core. An important feature is that the Somakoi basin culture has a well developed blade technology. The site wise distribution and analysis of artefacts of the Neolithic culture are represented in tabular form, in which the mean metric measurements, mean ratio and its percentage with raw material is discussed. A careful observation of these artefacts shows that flaked and chipped variety are mainly collected. The different size range and raw material of neolithic typology is represented in a tabular form. The dominant variety of raw material is dolerite. As per finished and semi-finished artefacts, axe and ring stone are the two dominant types of artefacts. Like other North Odisha site Telkoi site has reveals neolithic associate with ceramics. The materials are closely similar to those of Bajpur, Kamparkala, Bonaigarh cultural assemblages because these sites fall in the same region.

The chapter-IV, includes the aim and objectives of trial excavation, selection of site, analysis of lithic materials and ceramics, soil analysis etc, have been discussed to understand and interpret the causes of change and process cultural evolution, if any. The site of historical periods and their material culture were discussed. A good quality of ceramic remains of historical period is also discussed and reported different type pot, storage jar, lid, bowl etc.

The chapter-V includes general observation and conclusion, inter-relationship between sites, comparisons with surrounding areas of other sites and comparision with Kamparkala materials.

Scope for future work:

With view to the above attempt there are limitations to the present work so a good scope of work in this region is still waiting for. Very few number of Upper Palaeolithic tools have been reported from this survey. More survey in relation of other streams and channels may yield more evidence. Too much fragile ceramic is associated with ground and polishing stone culture (Neolithic Culture) with Telkoi site required more intensive survey in this locale to draw ceramic data base of the Neolithic period. Problem oriented excavation of sites belonging to different period is the need of the hour to rewrite historicity of this region of Odisha. Attempt should be made for recovery of Chalcolithic period site and Iron Age sites. Although the present survey has resulted one historical sites considered to be belonging medieval period. So attempt of should also be made for the recovery of early historical site. The study area has been inhabited by tribal people so further study with an ethno-archaeological prospective could help interpret the archaeological data more meaningfully.

In a true sense, it is holistic approach towards the reconstruction of the cultural pattern of North Odisha. However, some more work has to be done, which in my opinion, should engage the attention of scholars.

Bibliography

Acharya, P. 1923-29 *Annual Report of the Archaeological Survey of India*. pp. 100-101.

Acharya, P. and R.P. Chanda, 1930 Exploration in Orissa. *Memories of Archaeological Survey of India*, Calcutta.

Acharya, P. 1953 Catalogue of prehistoric tools, Archaeology section, Orissa state museum, Bhubaneswar.

Agrawal, D. P. 1982 Archaeology of India, Scandinavian Institution of Asian studied monograph series No.46, London: Curzon press limited.

Allchin, F.R. 1984 *Archaeology of India*. Select Book Service Syndicate, New Delhi.

Anderson, C.W, 1917 'Notes on prehistoric stone implements found in the singhbhum district', JBORS, Patna, Vol-III, Part-III, pp-349-362.

Ball, V. 1876 On stone implements found in the tributary states of Orissa. *Proceeding of the Asiatic Society of Bengal* (1876), pp.120-121.

Banarji, C. S. 1870 Notes on the antiquities of the Nalti, the Asia, and the Mahabinayaka hills of Cuttack. *Journal of the Asiatic Society of Bengal* 39 (part-I):158-171.

Basa, K.K. 1994 *Problems and Perspectives in Archaeology of Orissa*, Occasional Paper, DSA in Anthropology, Utkal University, Bhubaneswar, India.

Basa, K.K. 1997 Archaeological Heritage, Comprehensive history and culture of Orissa, Vol-I, edited by P.K Mishra and J.K Samal, New Delhi, Kaveri Books:18-45.

Basa, K.K , T.K. Das and B.K. Mohanta 2000 Neolithic Culture of Pallahara, Central Orissa. In K.K. Basa and P. Mohanty (edited) *Archaeology of Orissa*, pp. 264-84.

Behera, P.K. 1989 *Archaeology of Sundergarh District with special reference to the Brahmani Valley, Orissa*. Unpublished Ph.D Thesis, Banaras Hindu University, Varanasi.

Behera, P.K. 1991-92 Sulabhdihi: A Neolithic Celt Manufacturing Centre in Orissa. *Puratattava* 22: 124-132.

Behera, P.K. 1992 The Pebble Tool Component of the Bonaigarh Neolithic Complex, Orissa. *Man and Environment*, 18(2):57-63.

Behera, P.K. 2000 Neolithic Culture Complex of Bonaigarh Orissa. In Basa, K.K. and P. Mohanty edited *Archaeology of Orissa,* Pratibha Prakashan, New Delhi, Vol-I, pp. 222-263.

Beeching, 1868 Proceeding of the Asiatic society of Bengal, p-177.

Biswas, S. K. 1918 Indian Antiquary, Vol-.XLVII, pp-135-36.

Bose, N.K. and D. Sen, 1948 *Excavation in Mayurbhanj*. Calcutta: University of Calcutta.

Burkit, M.C. 1955 *The Old Stone Age Tools* (3rd edition), Cambridge.

Chakrabarti, S., D.K. Bhatacharya and D.K Chakrabarti 1982, The context of microliths at Paruldanga, Santiniketan, Man and Environment 6; 150- 52.

Chakravarty, M. 1967, Occurrence of Neolithic implements in West Bengal, Bull Cultural Research Institute, Vol-1 &2 , p-103.

Chakraborti, S. 2000 Recent Advances in Prehistory of Mayurbhanj. In K. K. Basa and P. Mohanty (edited) *Archaeology of Orissa*, Vol.1, pp. 77-101.

Chaulay. M.K. 2008 Prehistory and Protohistory of Eastern India, Agam Kala Prakashan, Delhi.pp-94-95

Das, T.K. 1995 *Surface Exploration Around Pallahara*, Unpublished M.A. dissertation, Department of Anthropology, Utkal University. Bhubaneswar.

Das, B. B. 1989 *Shri Bhanja Bhumi Kendujhari* (In Oriya), Barbil: Neelachal Prakashani.

Dash, R.N. 1987-88 *Neoliths of Orissa*, Unpublished Ph.D. Thesis, Utkal University, Bhubaneswar.

Dash, R.N. 2000 The Neolithic Culture of Orissa: A Typo-technological Analysis. In K. K. Basa and P. Mohanty (edited) *Archaeology of Orissa*, pp. 201-21.

Dasgupta, P. C, 1966 Archaeological Discoveries in west Bengal, Alipore: West Bengal Government Press.

Dehuri, R. 1997 *Archaeological Excavation at Kamparkala, Central Orissa*. Unpublished M.A. dissertation, Department of Anthropology, Utkal University. Bhubaneswar.

Dehuri, R. 1998 *Prehistoric Culture Around Telkoi, District: Keonjhar, Orissa*. Unpublished M.Phil. dissertation, Department of Anthropology, Utkal University. Bhubaneswar.

Dehuri, R. 2004 Paleo Relics around Telkoi, Dist- Keonjhar. *In Orissa Historical Research Journal*, Orissa State Museum, Bhubaneswar. Vol-XLVII, 4, pp.68-71.

Dehuri, R. 2011 Microlithic Culture around Kakharua Valley, North Central Orissa. *Kosala* 4, pp.100-106.

Dehuri, R. 2012 Some evidences of Neolithic remains around Kakharua valley in North Central Orissa, A preliminary study. *Kosala* 5, pp.71-78.

Dehuri, R. 2019 Archaeology of Eastern India, Agam Kala Prakashan, New Delhi.

Foote, R.B. 1987 Notes on Some Recent Neolithic and Palaeolithic in South India. *Journal of the Asiatic Society of Bengal*, Vol. LV: 92:259-282.

Ghosh, A.K. 1961 Prehistoric Studies in Eastern India. *Science and Culture*, 27 (8), pp.36-75.

Ghosh, A.K., 1970 The Palaeolithic Cultures of Singhbhum, TAPS, Philadelphia, p-6.

Indian Archaeology: A review 1959-60, pp-12-14.

Indian Archaeology: A review 1966-67.

Kar, S.K., K.K. Basa, and P.P Joglekar. 1998 Explorations at Gopalpur, District -Nayagarh, Coastal Orissa. *Man and Environment*, 23 (I), pp.107-114.

Kar, S.K. With an appendix by P.P. Joglekar. 2000 Gopalpur: A Neolithic-Chalcolithic site in Coastal Orissa. In K. K. Basa and P. Mohanty (edited) *Archaeology of Orissa,* pp. 368-91.

Khilar, B. K. 1997-99 Lithic Cultures around Deo River Basin, Orissa. *Manav*, (Paleo-culture special), 6, pp.73-76.

Krishnaswami, V. D, 1953 Progress in prehistoric, Ancient India, No-9, Plate-XV, New Delhi, pp.77-78.

Mishra, S.K. 1987-88 Stone Age Antiquities of Joshipur, Orissa – A Survey. *Man in Society*, 3, pp.81-88.

Mishra, S. 1997 *Surface Exploration around Kantala, Angul District, Orissa*. Unpublished M.A. dissertation, Department of Anthropology, Utkal University, Bhubaneswar.

Misra, V.N. 1962, Problems of terminology in Indian Prehistory. *Eastern Anthropologist,* XV (2), pp.112-124.

Mitra, D. and Chakravarti, D.K. 1958-59 Exploration in District Mayurbhanj, *Indian Antiquary*, p. 38.

Mitra, P. 1929 Prehistoric India, Calcutta.

Mohanta, B.K. 1995 *Archaeological Excavation at Bajpur (Pallahara), Orissa*. Unpublished M.A. dissertation, Department of Anthropology, Utkal University, Bhubaneswar.

Mohanta, B.K. 1997 *Surface Survey and Excavation of Muganali, Angul, Orissa.* Unpublished M.Phil dissertation, Department of Anthropology, Utkal University, Bhubaneswar.

Mohanty, P. 1985 The Mesolithic culture of Keonjhar District, Orissa: a preliminary report. *Bulletin of the Deccan College Post Graduate and Research Institute*, 44, pp.103-112.

Mohanty, P. 1989 *Mesolithic Settlement System of Keonjhar District, Orissa*. Unpublished Ph.D. Thesis submitted to the University of Poona, Pune.

Mohanty, P. 1991 The Mesolithic Culture of Keonjhar District. *Orissa Review*, September Issue, pp.4-7.

Mohanty, P. 1992 Stone Age Research in Orissa: An Overview. *Man in India*, 72(2), pp. 207-232.

Mohanty, P. 1998 The Mesolithic Culture of Keonjhar District, Orissa: A New Perspective. In Dutta, A. (edited) *New Perspective in History and Archaeology of Eastern India*. New Delhi: Books and Books.

Mohanty, P. 2000 Mesolithic Culture and Ethnography of Keonjhar District, Orissa. In K. K. Basa and P. Mohanty (edited) *Archaeology of Orissa*, pp. 114-52

Mohanty, P. and B. Tripathi. 1997-98 The Prehistoric, Proto historic and the Early Historic Cultures of Orissa. *Pragdhara* 8, pp.69-98.

Mohanty, D. 1999 *Archaeological Exploration around Sankerjang District; Angul, Orissa.* Unpublished M. A. Dissertation, Department of Anthropo- logy, Utkal University, Bhubaneswar.

Mahapatra G.C. 1985 The lower Palaeolithic in India. In (pp. 1-8) K.N Dikshit (edited) *Archaeological perspective of India since independence*, New Delhi: Books & Books.

Mohapatra, G.C. 1958-59 Exploration in Districts Keonjhar and Mayurbhanj. *Indian Antiquiry*, pp. 36-38.

Murray, E.F.O, 1941, The ancient workers of western Dhalbhum, JASB, 6,2 pp-61-104.

Murty, M.L.K.1985 Upper Palaeolithic Culture in India. In K.N. Dikshit edited *Archaeological Perspective of India Since Independence,* Books and Books, New Delhi, pp. 15-25.

Nayak, S. 1999 *Excavation at Sankerjang, District-Angul, Orissa.* Unpublished M. A. Dissertation, Department of Anthropology, Utkal University, Bhubaneswar, Orissa.

Ota, S.B. 1986 Mesolithic culture of the Phulbani District, Orissa with special reference to the heavy duty tool component. *Bulletin of the Deccan college post graduate and Research Institute* 45, pp.47-56.

Piggott, S. 1950 *Prehistoric India.* Harmondsworth: Penguin. Raychaudhury. P. C, 1985 Bihar district Gazetteers – Singhbhum, Patna, p-63.

Roy, R. 1994Some observation on the prehistoric sites in the vicinity of Pallahara, in Bio-cultural frontiers of Man and development (edited) N.K Behura and K.C. Tripathy, New Delhi, Mital Publication.

Roy, G. S. and Ray, A. 1963 'A technical study of some prehistoric potsherds,' Man in India, Vol-43.No-2, pp-147-149.

Sahoo, D. 2013 Archaeology before history at Kardi, District-Boudh. *SEARCH, A Journal of Arts, Humanities and managements* 1:86-103.

Senapati, N. 1986 *Orissa District Gazetteers: Keonjhar.* Cuttack: Orissa Government Press,

Singh, P.K. 1985 *Palaeoanthropology of Central Orissa.* Unpublished Ph.D. Thesis, Utkal University, Bhubaneswar.

Singh, P.K. 1988 Cultural succession of prehistoric culture in central Orissa. In K.L. Bhowmik (edited) *Cultura of the Past.* New Delhi: Inter India Publication. pp.87-99.

Singh, P.K. 1988-89 Neolithic Culture of Central Orissa. *Manav* 3, pp.275-281.

Singh, P.K. 2000 Stone Age Cultures of Central Orissa. In K. K. Basa and P.K Mohanty (edited) *Archaeology of Orissa.* pp. 102-13.

Sinha, S.C, 1951 The Discovery of some prehistoric stone tools in south manbhum, Science and culture;17, p-164.

Sen, D. 1969 Profile of a preliterate culture in the Sanjay valley, Singhbhum, Journal of Indian Anthropological Society, Vol-IV, pp-17-29.

Sen, D, and Ghosh A. K, 1960 'On the occurrence of Palaeoliths in Singhbhum, Man in India, Vol-40, No-3, pp-81-83.

Sen, D and Chaturvedi, U, 1957 Microlithic Industry of Singhbhum, Man in India, Vol-37, No-4, Ranchi, pp-294-305.

Thapar, B.K. 1985a Fresh Light of the Neolithic Cultures of India. In K.N Dikshit (edited) *Archaeological Perspective of India Since Independence*. pp. 37-43.

Tripathy, B. 2000 Archaeology of Boudh; Central Orissa. In K. K. Basa and P. Mohanty (edited) *Archaeology of Orissa*. pp.392-417

Tripathy, K.C. 1973 South Orissa Prehistory- the first record of stone age tools. *Asian Perspective* 4: 47-59.

Tripathy, K.C. 1980 *Lithic Industries in India: A Study of South Western Orissa*. Delhi: Leeladevi Publications.

Varma, R.K. 1985 The Mesolithic cultures of India. In K.N. Dikshit (edited) *Archaeological perspective of India since Independence*, Books & Books, New Delhi, pp. 27-36.

Worman, Jr. Eugene C. 1949 The Neolithic Problem in the Prehistory of India. *Journalof the Washington Academy of Science* 39 (6), pp.181-201.

INDEX

T

U

W

Plates

Pl. 1: General view of the Madhusudanpur locality-1.

Pl. 2: Grid and recording its materials at Telkoi site.

Pl. 3: Trial excavation Trench-R1 (2 x 2 m) at Telkoi site.

Pl. 4: Sieving of excavated soil from Trial trench, Telkoi site.